Culture, Self, and Meaning

Victor de Munck
State University of New York College, New Paltz

WAVELAND

PRESS, INC.

Prospect Heights, Illinois

For information about this book, write or call:
Waveland Press, Inc.
P.O. Box 400
Prospect Heights, Illinois 60070
(847) 634-0081
www.waveland.com

Contents

iii

Acknowledgments

The creation of a book is a mysterious and paradoxical process. On the one hand, it is very much the creation of the author, the individual who, one hopes, spins intricate and insightful webs of significance. The author dominates, indeed, makes the scene. On the other hand, it is astounding the extent to which the author (at least *this* author) is an intermediary, a henchman, and interloper in the begetting of a book.

There is Tom Curtin, the editor at Waveland, whose advice, patience, cajoling, encouragement, and enthusiasm kept me on track, moving, however lurchingly, forward. Doug Raybeck, who was writing a book at the same time, and I entered into a friendly competition to see who would finish first (he won). This ridiculous albeit friendly competition provided a wee bit o' turbocharge that both of us welcomed.

Academically, I owe a great debt to Theodore Schwartz, a man I deeply admire and who was (and remains) ahead of his time. Roy D'Andrade, Mel Spiro, Freddy Bailey, and Gananath Obeyesekere were undergraduate teachers who have continued to have a tremendous influence on my ideas and understanding of what it means to be human. David Kronenfeld and Alan R. Beals remain mentors and, now, colleagues who have unique minds. If it is true that one sees farther because one stands on the shoulders of giants, then I still have a lot of climbing to do.

The Anthropology Department and administration at SUNY–New Paltz has been generous and supportive, providing me with a relaxed and human enough environment that I did not feel the urge to write because otherwise I would perish. This seems to be a rare phenomenon these days.

But most of all there is my wife, Trini, who read, critiqued, edited, argued, and worked on this book nearly as many hours as I did.

Chapter One

Surveying the Terrain

All anthropology is psychological.
                    —Philip Bock
All psychology is cultural.
                    —Philip Bock
Culture and psychology make each other up.
                    —Richard A. Shweder and Maria A. Sullivan

There is truth to the above statements, but there is also a disconcerting everything and nothing quality to them. Anthropology and psychology are distinct and are considered to be two different academic disciplines. To a Westerner, culture is often pictured as part of the environment: one lives *in* culture. However, at the same time, we consider the
"self" to be a conscious entity that is separate from culture; self and culture are different conceptual units. The "self" is composed of psychological stuff: consciousness, a subconscious, ideas, thoughts, feelings, a personality. Culture is composed of rituals, life cycles, norms, and values: all
of the things that are external to us. In short, culture is out there and
psychology is in here.

The above quotation from Shweder and Sullivan (1993) acknowledges that culture and psychology are distinct, but that how and where
to mark the division is unclear. If culture and psychology "make each
other up," then they are each other's creation and creators: a logically
disconcerting concept. Does it all occur in a mad whirlwind of simulta-
neous activity, like two cartoon characters enveloped in a roiling cloud of
dust? Or is it a work in progress?

Obviously, one does not exist as a psyche—a self—outside of culture; nor does culture exist independent of its bearers. While we depend
on both our cultural and natural environments for survival, the two are
fundamentally different kinds of environments. Culture would cease to
exist without the individuals who make it up, but the natural environ-

1

ment would continue without us. Culture requires our presence as individuals. With this symbiosis, self and culture together make each other up and, in that process, make meaning.

I have organized this book around three questions: (1) Where is culture located? (2) What is the self? and (3) What is meaning? Each chapter presents a broad-ranging, ambitious discussion of different theoretical positions on these questions. I have written these chapters as independent sections so that teachers and readers need not read the book as a lineally structured narrative but can move about as they see fit. However, let me add that I consider "culture, self, and meaning" to be indisputably and irrevocably interconnected as a kind of theoretical triad. We cannot, for example, speak of culture without also recruiting our notions of self and meaning. Anthropologists are fond of saying that culture shapes the self, but selves are also the bearers of culture, and what is born and supported by us as cultured selves is, of course, meaning.

I am a cognitive anthropologist fascinated by the perplexing question of what it is to be human. The cognitive perspective of anthropology (as I see it) seeks to illuminate a part of this mystery by examining the dynamic between the conscious self and culture, without (I should add) knowing quite how culture and self articulate or, indeed, exactly what they are. This is precisely what makes anthropology and specifically, cognitive anthropology, fascinating—culture and self become the subjects of inquiry rather than default explanations for human behavior.

My background as a cognitive anthropologist helps explain what was selected for inclusion and what was excluded in this book. Cognitive anthropologists study culture and meaning by trying to find out what is going on in the mind of a person. The mind of a person does not exist outside a self—this includes a body and a psyche. Culture, self, and meaning are inextricably linked; they are different facets, different faces, of what it is to be human.

The part culture plays in shaping our understandings and theories of the self and of meaning cannot be ignored. Few people would question the statement that cultures are different. But the very simplicity of this truism conceals such mysteries that it implodes on closer examination. For example, if cultures differ, then they must be bounded wholes, like nations; so then, where does one culture begin and end? Where is it? What differences are we referring to? We know that members of our own culture hold very different political ideologies, beliefs, values, and goals. Some people in the United States lack ambition, some are obsessively ambitious; some have a sense of humor, others are humorless. Yet we classify them as members of the same American culture. How are they the same? What does it mean to say American culture, or Japanese culture, or, for that matter, Black culture? Is Justice Clarence Thomas a member of Black culture?

The first chapter, on culture, will undoubtedly be my most controversial chapter. I have divided theories of culture into inside and outside perspectives of culture. By "inside" I mean that culture is considered to be located and constructed in the minds of individuals. By "outside" I mean that the researcher looks for culture in public life and in those symbols, structures, and processes that shape and constrain our behaviors. This distinction is mostly for heuristic purposes. Few theories of culture have ever been purely inside or outside theories. Inside theories must, of course, consider the effects of the outside world on shaping the inside world, and vice versa. Nevertheless, I argue that there is a profound difference between inside and outside theories of culture. The former address diversity within rather than between cultures, and the latter emphasize diversity between and uniformity within cultural populations.

In his article "Writing for Culture," Christoph Brumann also used a similar conceptual division to classify different theories of culture. He distinguishes between those that focus on culture as bounded and uniform (what I collapse under the label "superorganic") and those that view culture as variable and contingent (1999:S1). Brumann's purpose is to criticize those anthropologists who advocate abandoning the concept of culture altogether and to show why the concept is valuable. He argues that we should retain the concept mostly on pragmatic grounds, as it is being co-opted by other disciplines.

In his editorial to the special issue in *Current Anthropology* titled "Culture—A Second Chance?" Richard Fox, the editor, writes:

> In recent years, the culture concept has gained wide (and vapid) usage in popular expression, for example in common terms such as "corporate culture," the "culture" of schools, and "the culture wars." A more insidious recent usage occurs when supposed irreconcilable differences in "culture" are used to justify an anti-immigrant or anti-minority politics. (1999:i)

At the conclusion of the chapter on culture, I discuss the implications of inside and outside perspective of culture on popular conceptions of culture and public policy. I argue, with Brumann, that anthropologists do have important things to say about culture and that to reject or discard the term because of its elitist and essentialist under- (and sometimes, over-) tones is not only plain stupid but ultimately irresponsible, because it encourages power mongers and fanatics to inflate and essentialize what Sigmund Freud referred to as "the narcissism of minor differences."

I have included a discussion on the psychological and cultural importance of social networks in the chapter on culture. The benefit of this idiosyncratic inclusion outweighs the risks because social network studies are becoming increasingly more sophisticated and prominent in sociology (Sanjek 1990:397) and in studies of corporate culture, globalization, and transnationalism (Hannerz 1996). Anthropologists were among the first to adopt and use network analysis for fieldwork research. Where once we were central players in this interdisciplinary field, we are now marginalized. My brief discussion of a few of the important cultural and psychological effects of network shapes, sizes, and positions is easy to follow and intended to help reintroduce these ideas into our discourses on culture.

My discussion of Theodore Schwartz's (1978) idea of the "idioverse"—that each individual has his or her own version of culture—will not be found in other nonspecialized psychological anthropology books. However, Schwartz's idea that culture is "cognitively distributed" among the members of a culture is voiced by many scholars of culture who claim it as their own idea. Further, this is the theoretical approach that is best developed by anthropologists and one that "we" can claim and use to contribute to the current popular debates over what "culture" is.

Brumann points out that "outside anthropology and academia the word [culture] is gaining popularity" while, at the same time, many anthropologists have called for "abandoning the concept" (1999:S1). I argue that, at present, Schwartz provides the most coherent and complete theory of culture as "contingent" and "variable." Though not included in this book, the works of Kim Romney and his associates on consensus analysis offer a methodology to complement Schwartz's theoretical position.

My inclusion of network and idioverse theory is unusual in an introductory text. Reflexively considered, the inclusion of these theories signals my optimism that there is currently a renewed interest among students and anthropologists in an unapologetic empirical anthropology. By introducing these ideas, readers will have added new living tools to their repertoire for thinking and talking about culture.

The chapters on the self and meaning are less controversial. The chapter on the self profiles the development of Western ideas about the self, particularly in terms of the distinctions made between the "I" and "me," and the private and public aspects of the self. Cross-cultural studies of the self are also discussed. It has been posited that the Western concept of the self is different than non-Western cultural concepts of the self. I present the issues involved in this debate and discuss three well-known comparative studies of the self.

The chapter on meaning relies on cognitive models of meaning. This chapter traces the development of theories of meaning from the 1950s to the present. In the 1960s, cognitive anthropology was a bustling and dynamic field and led to advances in our understanding of such universal cognitive structures as taxonomies, paradigms, and marking hierarchies. Anthropologists were considered important "players" in the emerging field of cognitive science. However, through the 1970s and most of the 1980s cognitive anthropology was left for dead, as interpretivist and postmodern positions came to the ascendancy. However, the field was never quite "dead." Many of its practitioners worked in interdisciplinary cognitive science departments (particularly the University of California at Irvine) or published in psychology journals. Cognitive anthropology was officially resurrected in 1987 with the publication of *Cultural Models in Language and Thought*, edited by Dorothy Holland and Naomi Quinn. Since that time it has continued to grow, mostly as an interdisciplinary field that straddles anthropology and psychology, without being a fully accepted member of either discipline.

The text you are about to read is broad in scope and ambition. It is pitched at a level that challenges but is accessible to the undergraduate and novice graduate student. I have also tried to write this book from the point of a teacher preparing lectures. I expect that instructors and students will readily recognize the gist of each position presented and expand on or bring other arguments to bear.

Chapter Two

Where Is Culture Located?

Answer one: Culture is located out there, in the public world.

Answer two: Culture is located in here, in the private sphere of the self.

Where culture *is* also suggests what it *does*. If culture is located in the mind, then we, as individuals, make up our own culture. If culture is located outside, then we, as cultural animals, are made up by culture. There is, of course, a middle position, that "the locus of culture [is] inherently ambiguous and [can]not be adequately characterized in exclusively psychological or social terms" (Shore 1996:51). Few anthropologists would disagree with Bradd Shore's statement, though some will argue that the term "culture" itself is so closely associated with colonialism and essentialist characterizations of the "primitive" and "exotic Other" that it is forever tainted and should be dropped from the lexicon, preferably with cement boots into the ocean depths. However, excising culture from anthropology is a bit like biologists denying evolution.

Shore's point is that culture has no central locus and no consistent molecular (i.e., conceptual) structure. Culture overlaps with both psychological (such as personality and motivations) and sociological (such as family or occupational relations) aspects of human life, but it is also something else. Some of those "something elses" and how they combine with psychological and sociological concepts are discussed in this chapter. I begin by presenting various theories that consider culture to be located outside the person in the public realm of life. This is followed by discussions of theories locating culture in the individual, mostly in the mind, as ways of knowing and desiring. I will conclude with an examination of the implications of these two perspectives on how people think about culture and how these perspectives may influence public policy. This section pro-

7

vides the proper forum for addressing questions regarding whether the concept of culture should be discarded or whether we should reconceive culture as an adjective (i.e., cultural) or plural noun (cultures) in order to trash the notion of cultures as homogeneous, static, and bounded wholes.

Answer one, that culture is located "outside, in the public world," is the most common answer given by anthropologists, sociologists, and ordinary folk. There are different versions of the "outside" doctrine, but, by virtue of externalizing culture relative to the individual, all proponents of this view share certain assumptions that have important implications for how we think about culture and, ultimately, for how we shape a national culture. I will discuss three versions of the culture-is-outside answer: the *superorganic*, the *interpretivist*, and the *social structural*.

Answer two, that culture is located inside—in the mind—is most strongly advocated by cognitive anthropologists. This position holds that culture, in any real (see it, touch it) sense, does not exist. Rather, culture, like the design of a car seat, designates an *average* of some population's set of beliefs, values, and knowledge. From this perspective, psychology refers to the mental characteristics of any one person while culture refers to the generic attributes of those characteristics that are shared by other members of society.

I will describe three theoretical positions for the inside view: (1) the psychoanalytic as presented by Melford Spiro, a strong advocate for the psychic unity of humankind; (2) a symbolic-psychoanalytic approach developed by Gananath Obeyesekere, who holds a "militantly-middle position" (Fernandez and Herzfeld, 1998:94) in which he combines interpretivist and psychoanalytic approaches; and (3) Ted Schwartz's theory of "distributive" culture based on the concept of the idioverse.

CULTURE IS LOCATED OUTSIDE

Version 1: Culture Is Superorganic

"Organic" means that culture is alive, has form, feelings, skills, and purposes. "Super" does not refer to a quality, but rather to culture as an organism that exists at a higher level of abstraction than the individual; the relationship of culture to humans is analogous to that of a human being to her cells. The superorganic perspective personifies cultures and holds that for each culture there exists a set of people—the members of that culture—that are unique and distinct from members of all other cultures. The superorganic position was first presented by Alfred Kroeber (1909) who borrowed the term from Herbert Spencer (1876).

Few anthropologists explicitly advocate a superorganic view of culture. Nevertheless, Benjamin Colby and Lore M. Colby write that "even today . . . the great majority of anthropological writings on culture reflects an underlying superorganic bias" (1981:11; see also Bidney 1967:34). To illustrate, in a short and otherwise excellent book on ethnography, I came upon the following: "culture turns you into a fully-human being"; "culture defines you; it mentally imprisons you"; "culture also liberates you"; "your culture provides the perspective from which you view the world" (Bohannan and van der Elst 1998:7). These statements are easy to make because, though logically flawed, they *seem* intuitively right.

However fragmented and divided national cultures may be, they are, in part, composed of shared everyday experiences and national ceremonial cycles that help create an "imagined" national culture (Anderson 1987). For example, New Year's Day, the Super Bowl, Fourth of July, Thanksgiving and Christmas are ritual indices that mark, whether we favor them or not, the life cycle of U.S. national culture. Grocery shopping, eating cereal or eggs for breakfast, and public schooling are other common experiences shared by Americans whether they live in Florida or Montana. Though national borders are increasingly porous, individuals who have migrated elsewhere often retain, if not fervently embrace, their cultural identity. There is a "mother" culture that we identify with that is not erased when we move across national borders, and that feeling of identification often intensifies over time. The superorganic speaks to that kind of cultural essentialism.

If culture is a mega-entity, a biosphere, that houses and sustains us with its symbolic, social and material resources, then we are "compiled" by cultural programs. We are our culture, just as one might say "We are what we eat." Ruth Benedict (1959) used the "seductive metaphor" of a circle and arc to describe possible cultural "configurations." Each culture is represented by an arc of the circle, and members of a culture absorb and reflect the properties that emanate from their specific cultural arc.[1]

Using a more contemporary metaphor, Claudia Strauss (1992a:9) refers to this perspective as the "fax model" of culture. A culture copies itself onto our respective biological sheets and we, as the bearers of that culture, "fax" it to our children. Shore (1996:7) notes that a superorganic view of culture logically entails that the mind is a "passive recording device "into which information is "dumped" and stored. Culture is active; psychology is passive. The primary functions of a culture are to sustain and reproduce itself (perhaps it is not just individuals who have a libido!).

Superorganic theory emphasizes cultural variation and, traditionally, has been implicitly accepting of a view of the "psychic unity of humankind." Psychic unity is, or has been, a *foundational axiom* of anthropology. This axiom is grounded in the belief that, except for cultural differences, human beings everywhere are fundamentally alike in terms of mental and physical capacities. Significant variations are a consequence of different cultural histories and different adaptations to different physical environments.

By anthropomorphizing culture, individual cultures inevitably become described in terms of emotional and personality patterns, referred to as the "ethos" of a culture. The cultural ethos is then faxed onto the members of the culture as "personality"; faxing is accomplished through institutionalized socialization practices. For example, the generational faxing of traditional American beliefs about the rational male and the compassionate-relational female is illustrated in the following story about role assignment and choice taken from Douglas Hofstadter (1995). Elementary school students from an elite neighborhood were taken to a hospital where the girls were given nurses' caps and boys were given stethoscopes. The parents complained, arguing that the hospital staff was reinforcing sexist stereotypes. The next year a new batch of students went to the hospital. Again all the girls wore nursing caps and the boys stethoscopes. This time when the parents complained, the teachers and hospital staff replied that they had given the children the choice to choose one or the other, and that is what the children chose.

I began this discussion by arguing that few, if any, anthropologists are explicit advocates of a superorganic approach and that we effortlessly slip into talking about culture as if it were alive. By investing culture with goals, emotions, and ideas, we simultaneously tend to view the human psyche as a tabula rasa upon which these cultural configurations are inscribed. There are clues by which we can detect this kind of analogical slippage. For example, when the word "culture" is used as a mass noun followed by an active verb, it is implied that culture acts, as in the statement "culture represses the individual." A second clue occurs when some essential quality or trait (e.g., "American culture is patriarchal") is used to describe an entire culture. Third, the superorganic view presumes that the psyche (by and large) is a cultural construct; thus culture and people are frequently connected by a prepositional clause, as in the phrase: "if you were raised in a different culture" (Bohannan and van der Elst 1998:7). Remarks such as "Americans are ambitious and materialistic," "Chinese are inscrutable," "men are from Mars and women are from Venus," "Jews are intelligent," and "the old are so conservative" invoke the superorganic view of culture. It is for this reason that Robert Borofsky (following Roger M. Keesing) writes, "I use the term 'cultural' rather than 'culture.' The adjectival form downplays culture as some innate essence, as some living material thing" (1994:245).[2] Consequently Lila Abu-Lughod argues that "Perhaps anthropologists should consider strategies for writing against culture" (1991:147). Abu-Lughod argues that even if the author doesn't use "culture" to refer to some essential qualities of a group of people, the term carries too much essentialist baggage to ignore, and therefore we are better off without it.

Version 2: Culture Is Public

Arguably the best-known anthropologist of our day, Clifford Geertz, writes:

> Culture is public because meaning is. . . . to say that culture consists
> of socially established structures of meaning in terms of which people
> do such things as signal conspiracies and join them or perceive in-
> sults and answer them, is no more to say that it is a psychological
> phenomenon, a characteristic of someone's mind, personality, cogni-
> tive structure or whatever than to say that Tantrism, genetics, the
> progressive form of the verb, the classification of wines, the Common
> Law, or the notion of "a conditional curse" . . . is. (1973:12–13)

Geertz argues with the superorganic theorists that culture is
located outside the individual. However, for Geertz, culture consists of
symbols that convey meaning, and these symbols are located in the "public" arenas of life: "thinking consists not of 'happenings in the head' . . .
but of a traffic in significant symbols" (1973:45). These symbols are found
in public arenas: the "house yard," "marketplace," and "town square"
Note the shift in emphasis from what culture *does* to what it *is*. Culture
may be "outside," but the fallacy of animus, of insufflating the incorpo-
real with life, is eliminated. Meaning is public, and culture is the system
that packages meanings for people to use (i.e., to "signal conspiracies").

By arguing that thinking is a public act and that the content of the
human mind is made of cultural stuff, Geertz emphasizes the plasticity
of the human psyche rather than its unity (which he does not completely
reject). Shore observed that for Geertz, "Culture moves from the periph-
eries of human life into its very center as a postnatal completion of
human development. The study of human nature minus culture does not
produce a more basic understanding of human life, but an understanding of a protohuman" (1996:33). This asserts that any study of what it
means to be human, whether the focus is on the individual or the social,
must investigate culture, and culture consists of symbol systems, that is,
of "meaning."

Culture packages meaning in symbols, which Geertz calls "the
material vehicles of thought" (1973:362). By using "material vehicles,"
Geertz wants to emphasize, once more, that symbols, meaning, and culture are extrinsic to the mind and are open to inspection and study, just
as the human anatomy is inspected and studied. Geertz rejects the mind
as the locus of culture and upbraids anthropologists, particularly cognitive ones, who trivialize culture by "psychologizing" it. Though Geertz
acknowledges that all sense data are processed in "a secret grotto in the
head" (1973:362), he asserts that we cannot know what happens there.
All that we can ultimately know are the things people do in public places:
actions, as opposed to thoughts and feelings, are observable, describable,
and analyzable.

Geertz proposed an "experience near," "interpretivist" anthropology
that studies individuals-in-context where they "traffic" in discernible
symbols. Participants both produce and "read," or interpret, each other's
symbols. "Experience near" concepts refer to those concepts people use

"spontaneously, unselfconsciously, as it were colloquially; they do not, except fleetingly and on occasion, recognize that there are any 'concepts' involved at all" (Geertz 1984:125). For example, in the classroom the professor lectures and students listen, occasionally a student raises her hand to ask a question and a discussion may ensue. The students may feel confused, bored, or interested, but whatever one feels, however one evaluates the situation, the various "traffic in symbols" is read spontaneously. We do not ask ourselves, "do I raise my hand to ask a question?" But we may ask ourselves, "do I want to raise my hand?"

The interpretivist position is really very different from the superorganic. Here, there is no super organism, no inclination to describe culture as a prime mover causing people to do things. Geertz's emphasis is on cultures-in-specific rather than "culture-in-general."[3] Culture is not a mysterious superentity nor is it a dwarf inside the head frantically processing, storing and launching information down the neural pipeline. Culture is here in front of our eyes, apparent in the bustle of transactions, managed through the shuffling back and forth of little packages of meaning—symbols exchanged between people in public places.[4]

Culture, as Geertz defines it, is a "system of symbols," or, alternatively, "the webs of significance [man] has himself spun" (1973:5). The job of the anthropologist is to be able to interpret those symbols and tease out their meanings. The individual is not, as in the superorganic model, culture "writ small"; it is, rather, an active spinner of cultural webs. Geertz's position is also critical of the idea of anthropology as a scientific venture, for there may be many reasonable and plausible interpretations of the congeries of symbols that comprise any particular cultural text. In his own way, Geertz could be construed as an advocate for empiricism (the view that sensory experience is the only source of knowledge), for he entrusts the study of culture and the psyche to activities occurring in the phenomenal world. To posit either superorganic or psychological causes and goals is, to Geertz, indulging oneself in "what-if" fictions.

Version 3: The Size, Position and Strength of Social Networks
    "We live in society just as we live in our flesh" writes E. P. Thompson (1994:249). Society is made up of social roles, statuses and norms that create an *"ensemble* of . . . social relations" (1994:219; italics in original). Thus, to study humans as social animals we also need to attend to the structural configurations of those social ensembles. Unlike Geertz, such studies do not see culture as emanating from the mouths and bodies of people, but from the structural webbing (so to speak) that organizes the relationships between people.

One can analyze structures *sociocentrically* or *egocentrically*, at the macro or the micro level. "Sociocentrically" means that one investigates how social structures affect culture, personality, or economic, political, religious or social systems. For example, hierarchical social structures are also likely to produce cultural myths and values that validate the concentration of political power and wealth in the hands of a few.

Egocentric structural analyses are more user friendly for psychologists and anthropologists because they focus on small groups such as corporations, schools, or communities. In egocentric structural analysis, the focus is usually on how decision-making procedures, the flow of information, and a group culture are affected by structural properties. Critical to all structural analysis is that structures possess certain logical properties that constrain and shape the kinds of social exchanges, interactions, personalities, values, and beliefs of the social body.

Structures are a bit like ocean pier pilings on which people, like mussels, attach themselves. This metaphor is doubly suggestive, because it implies both that structure is the organizing principle of society and that individuals are not autonomous symbol-generating agents. A structural analysis is bewitchingly scientific because it promises to explain so much, so logically, from just a few elementary structural starting points. Bourdieu, falling under the structural spell, enthuses that only our pretensions keep us from agreeing with Leibniz that "we are automatons in three-quarters of what we do" (1984:474).[5] In other words, structure (anthropomorphized) dictates most of what we do, not some internal unique self.

I will discuss three properties of structures: *number, shape* and *strength*. My discussion is limited to small egocentric structures; my understanding of structures comes from studying social network analysis and not economic or political structures.

Number—From One To Many. Georg Simmel (1950) studied how the size and form of social structures shape cultural norms and psychological dispositions. He argued that behaviors and values vary significantly depending on whether an individual is (1) alone, (2) in a group of two—a dyad, (3) in a group of three—a triad, or (4) a member of a large group.

Simmel said that "pure freedom" is only possible when one is alone, for only in such a condition is it possible to satisfy personal preferences without having to accommodate other people's preferences. Being alone removes social constraints and empowers the individual to do what he wants to do. He can eat greasy pizza in bed, watch wrestling on TV, and burp without fear of reprimand. More virtuously, many cultures portray the world renouncer and the solitary traveler as icons of the free and unencumbered life.

Constraints present themselves once one enters the social realm. The minimal social unit is two people—the dyad.[6] The logical properties of the dyad entail that each individual is *equally* important for the maintenance of the group. They are equal in the sense that the death or departure of either member terminates the group. Because each is necessary for the existence of the group, the dynamics of dyadic relationships tend to be emotionally charged. Each individual assertion of a preference or desire automatically represents the interests of half the group. Consequently, group decisions tend to be based on subjective rather than objective criteria. To illustrate: if two friends are going out to a restaurant and one favors pizza and the other Chinese, then the person who expresses his preference most insistently is most likely to "win." Dyadic relations tend to coalesce around personal interests; preserving the group depends on satisfying the interests of the other person.

Emotional investment in a group correlates negatively with the number of people in that group: the larger the group, the less each individual's emotional investment in that group. Conversely, the smaller the group, the greater each individual's emotional investment in that group. Therefore, we can expect that relations in a dyad will be more intimate (i.e., more subjective) than relations in all other social groups.

In triads, each person constitutes one-third of the group. This is important because, unlike in dyads, no one person has the power to terminate the social unit by leaving. According to Simmel, this property of triads entails that group dynamics are characterized by "objective" rather than subjective criteria. Objective means that decisions are made according to cultural principles for what constitutes a reasoned argument. For example, if you have three friends, each wanting to eat at a different restaurant, then, for the good of the group, it is not a good strategy for one friend to harangue the others into eating at her favorite restaurant. This is so because the two friends can drop the haranguer and still maintain the "group." The survival of the group is no longer in the hands of the individual. If the group is to endure, then decisions such as where to eat should be reached by objective criteria (e.g., price, food preferences, proximity of the restaurants) that are considered "fair" or "equitable" by each member of the group.

In the metropolis, social distances between individuals are increased to the point that the vast majority of individuals are strangers to each other. Consequently, their emotional investment in each other is minimal, and their behaviors are reduced to and shaped by conventionalized emblems, signals, and functions. Increases in population also lead to deeper, more complex, hierarchical structures, and this in turn increases social, economic, knowledge, and skill differentiation. Building on Simmel's analysis, Peter Blau hypothesized that the "erosion of extended kinship is the result . . . of the sheer size of contemporary societies" (1977:134). The more humanity clumps together, like mussels on the pier pilings, the greater the ratio of strangers to acquaintances and family. This leads to a diminished psychic investment by individuals in social life, a cultural devaluation of civic values, and an increased psychic investment in, and cultural valuation of, family and voluntary associations.

The Shape of Social Structures. Structures have different shapes, and many structural theorists investigate the psychological and cultural effects of different structural shapes. This discussion focuses on the classic studies on communication networks conducted by Art Bavelas (1950) and his associates at M.I.T. Bavelas described four elementary structural shapes: circle, Y, horseshoe (or line), and star.[7] This discussion concerns itself only with the two extreme structural shapes—the circle and the star (see figure 1.1).

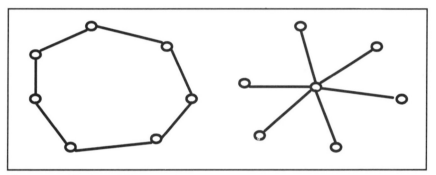

Figure 1.1. Circle and Star Graphs

Bavelas wanted to see what the effects of different structural (or social network) configurations were on how groups solve problems. In a series of laboratory experiments, seven students were placed in cubicles so that they could not see each other but could pass and receive notes through slots. Each group was given a problem to solve, and each participant received one piece of information. The experimenters let the members of the group communicate their information to others, either by passing within a circle or star formation. The experimenters evaluated the efficiency of the group in solving a problem by timing how long it took them to come up with an answer and whether the answer was right. In circle structures, it took six moves for everyone to receive all the information necessary to make the right decision. In star structures, the outside positions needed to make just one move to give all the information necessary to make the right decision to the person occupying the center position.

Star and circle networks differ not only in the means by which information is processed, but also in the level of participant satisfaction. The star networks were significantly quicker and more accurate in solving a series of problems because all the peripheral actors quickly realized that to "win," their best strategy was to pass their information to the person at the center. In circle networks, many more steps were needed. After six "passes," all of the circle participants received full information at the same time, and then discussions ensued, though they sometimes led to selecting the wrong answer.

In postinterviews, the participants in the circle network experiments reported that they had more difficulty figuring out the structure of their group, but they all enjoyed the task. Participants in the star networks became efficient problem solvers quickly, but only the central person reported a high satisfaction rating as a participant in the experiment. It was concluded that structural shapes are important in problem solving and that star-shaped (i.e., centralized) structures are more efficient than circle-shaped (i.e., egalitarian) structures. If the objective is to maximize the satisfaction of all the participants in a social group, then the optimal choice is circle-shaped structures. It seems that people can have efficient structures with mostly unhappy participants or inefficient structures with happy participants, but not both!

In a little-known follow-up study in the 1960s, Lois Rogge wondered to what extent location in a social structure shaped a person's personality.[8] She placed people who scored low on self-esteem and self-confidence in personality tests in the central position on star-shaped structures and those who scored high on self-esteem and self-confidence in the peripheral positions and ran the Bavelas experiment. Rogge had the participants return and repeated the experiment numerous times, each time with the participants remaining in their original positions. She found that, over time, the low-esteem folks became decisive, self-confident decision makers while the originally high-esteem folks became indecisive and less self-confident. From these experiments, she concluded that personality traits are, to a large extent, a function of the structural properties of social networks.

The Strength of Structural Ties. Mark Granovetter argued that cultural values and one's personal worldview are "bound up with larger-scale aspects of social structure, well beyond the purview or control of particular individuals" (1973:364). He investigated the ways in which the relative strength of personal ties influenced an individual's access to economic resources, especially job opportunities. The importance of the strength of ties on behavior rests on the observation that we behave differently with those we have a strong tie to than with those we have a weak tie to. Granovetter defined the "strength" of a social tie as "a combination of the amount of time, the emotional intensity, the intimacy (mutual confiding), and the reciprocal services which characterize the tie" (1973:348). He hypothesized that the stronger the tie between A and B, the more likely that their social networks will overlap; the weaker the tie, the less their social networks will overlap. Thus, if A and B have a strong tie and A has a strong tie with C, then B probably has a tie with C.

Weak ties, such as those with acquaintances or colleagues, generally involve only the occasional phone call or e-mail. These ties are "indispensable to an individual's opportunities" (p. 365) for two reasons: (1) those individuals you are connected to by weak ties are unlikely to have overlapping social networks; therefore, each weak tie connects you to a different social network, and (2) you do not need to invest much time and effort to maintain a weak tie. That is, weak ties maximize an individual's connections to the social world.

Strong ties involve what Alan Fiske (1991) has called "*communal sharing*" in which goods and information are distributed freely to in-members. Strong ties bind individuals to each other in webs of mutual obligations, duties, and dependencies. Strong ties are particularly important in groups where the members rely on one another for mutual economic, social, and political support. For example, strong ties often characterize relations among the poor in industrialized societies and in low-technological societies where individuals need to cooperate to get things done.

From a national cultural perspective, weak ties are vital for the overall integration of large-scale communities, cities, and nations. Through weak ties, it is possible to invoke the ideal of the "imagined community" (Anderson 1987) because they are the only possible ties that can be used symbolically to connect large and culturally diverse populations. Strong ties create strong local loyalties and cohesion but also lead to "overall fragmentation" because they turn the group inward and cannot be used to build "bridges" between communities (p. 365).

Structural positions intrigue me because they completely disregard the human element, the psyche, in explaining human behavior. Structural approaches pose the question "What can we explain about a person or group without taking the person or group into account?" By denying psychological variables and explanations, structural positions illuminate aspects of human life that would otherwise remain inaccessible. Psychological and structural approaches are alternative worldviews, somewhat analogous to those pictures in which one sees at one time a vase and another time a female profile, but never both simultaneously. Similarly, each approach provides a wholly other mode for viewing and understanding human life.

CULTURE IS LOCATED IN PEOPLE'S HEADS

Two psychoanalytic versions are examined here, one represented by Melford Spiro and the other by Gananath Obeyesekere. Spiro presents a theoretical framework that allows for cultural diversity and at the same time postulates a universal "human nature." Spiro's task is to explain how our common human nature projects out into the world and acts on our social-physical environment to produce culture.

Obeyesekere combines psychoanalytic and interpretivist approaches. He is concerned with how "traffic in public symbols" provides both the person and the public symbolic resources for interpreting and curing psychic afflictions. Obeyesekere's emphasis is on how the individual internalizes cultural (public) symbol systems.

Third, I will present the "idioverse" perspective of Theodore Schwartz. This approach seeks to explain culture as a "by-product" of the cumulative, shared experiences of individuals. The idea of culture as "by-product" or the "residual" of experience anticipates the current debates (discussed in the introduction) over whether anthropologists should banish the term "culture" from the discipline. By proposing that culture is derived from experience and not the other way around, Schwartz manages to explicitly and forcefully de-essentialize culture while still retaining it as a useful concept.

Version One: Spiro's Psychoanalytic and "Human Nature" Thesis of Culture

Over the course of fieldwork conducted in three very different cultures—a Micronesian atoll (Ifaluk), a Burmese village, and an Israeli kibbutz—Spiro made three important observations: (1) there are psychological similarities and differences between the members of a culture; (2) the range of psychological variability between people *within* a culture is as great, if not greater, than the range of psychological variability *between* cultures; and (3) there are significant psychological similarities between members of these very different cultures (1987:8). What to make of this?

Spiro rejected the strong cultural relativist/determinist position that all cultures are unique and that culture was "*the* determinant" of personality (1987:25; italics in original). He reasoned that if cultures are nonoverlapping, unique configurations (the strong cultural relativist position), then there should be no significant psychological similarities between people of different cultures. But there are, and therefore the strong cultural relativist position is false.

Instead, he argued, that culture was "*a* determinant" of personality (1987:25; italics in original). The psychological similarities he observed between groups was a result of "*human nature*" (p. 9; italics in original). By "human nature" Spiro means "those shared principles that govern the functioning of the mind" (p. 9). These "shared principles" are a consequence of both our species-specific biology and our shared cultural solutions to a set of universal problems that all human groups must adequately resolve. For example, all social groups must attend to the issue of the prolonged helplessness of children (p. 24). In every culture, enduring affective bonds must be established between parents and children. Shared principles refer to the existence of a "psychic unity of humankind" that is a result of both biological *and* cultural determinants.

Spiro also takes issue with the cultural relativist view that cultures are "arbitrary" creations. Arbitrary means that cultures vary in indeterminable ways, in much the same way that languages do. For example, there is no fundamental reason why "tree" is the English word and "*baum*" the German word for tree. The relationship between the sound, meaning, and actual referents is patterned but arbitrarily derived. To understand Spanish, for example, one should study Spanish in terms of its own phonetics, syntax, and meaning systems and not with reference to another language or some universal *ur*-language. Similarly, cultural relativists hold that cross-cultural differences in religious beliefs, marriage practices, food preferences, and so on are arbitrary. There is no primal and primary cultural template; nor is there any set of cultural evolutionary templates. Each culture offers "fundamentally different 'frames' for understanding" reality and there are as many realities as cultures" (Shweder and Bourne 1984:48).

Spiro rejects the idea of arbitrariness. He argues that the surface variations in cultures mask underlying similarities. For example, while not all cultures have a belief in witchcraft, all have some belief in supernatural beings, and this belief expresses our human need to explain misfortune "*in the absence of competitive explanations*" (1987:209; italics in original). More generally, Spiro posits that the variations in religious systems can still be distilled to a belief in superhuman beings and the rituals used to summon them. The belief in superhuman beings satisfies our universal "substantive desires" for such things as "rain, Nirvana, crops, heaven, victory in war, [and] recovery from illness" (p. 211). The concept of superhuman beings has its origins in the universal social institution, the family, in which children depend on their parents for their survival. For Spiro, cultures are systems that function to meet the psychological and biological requirements of human beings as members of society.

Version Two: Obeyesekere and Personal and Public Symbols
Most contemporary psychoanalytical anthropologists are confused about where culture is located and vacillate between asserting that culture is in or outside the body. For example, the box on the following page lists a number of definitions of culture taken from *Medusa's Hair: An Essay on Personal Symbols and Religious Experience* (1981) by Gananath Obeyesekere, probably the best-known psychoanalytic anthropologist of our time.

Clearly, Obeyesekere favors locating culture inside the individual. However, he also vacillates between defining culture as "a set of ideas" (a very passive rendering of culture) or as an agent ordering and giving coherence to the world, a variant of the superorganic position.

Definition 2 combines aspects of both the superorganic and Geertzian positions: culture acts (e.g., "confers," "mediates") on human perceptions, but it is also identified with public systems of meaning. The same point is made with definition 3, where Obeyesekere describes culture as a "set of meanings" that people use to "impose" meaning "on the world."

Definitions of Culture by Obeyesekere (1981)

1. "If culture consists of the ideas people have about their world, an anthropological theory is *our* conceptual and abstract rendering of *their* conceptual and abstract rendering of the world" (p. 10; italics in the original).

2. "[C]ulture confers meaning upon the formless, meaningless reality of the phenomenal world. I see the world out there physically, but my perceptions, even if organized, have no meaning unless mediated by culture" (p. 109). This is a paraphrase of Max Weber's definition of culture, which Obeyesekere approvingly quoted.

3. "The set of meanings that human beings impose on the word is what we mean by culture. Culture orders the world and gives it coherence and form" (p. 110).

4 "Culture consists of internalized ideas in the minds of men, which must therefore be mediated through consciousness" (p. 112).

5. "Cultural meanings such as those embodied in religion help Everyman, not just the philosophical or introspective individual, to ruminate on the nature of experience" (p. 114).

Psyche is separate from culture and uses culture, here perceived as passive, to make meaning—in the same way a painter uses paint to make a picture. But in the very next sentence, the roles are reversed and culture becomes active—it "orders." Culture now does much more than just "confer meaning"; it takes on superorganic characteristics. Definitions 4 and 5 seesaw between defining culture as a noun ("internalized ideas") and as the subject of an active verb ("help"). In comparing definition 4 with 2, we find "consciousness" substituted for "culture" as the "mediating" principle, indicating Obeyesekere's quandary in deciding what culture and psychology, respectively, do.

Obeyesekere views culture and psychology as distinct and dialectically related domains of life. But he vacillates between defining culture as a passive noun (e.g., "a list of meanings") or as an active verb (conferring, ordering and giving coherence to perceptions). As a passive noun, culture is unequivocally located inside the head, serving as symbolic grist for the psychic mill. As a verb, the relationship is reversed, and *experience* becomes grist for the cultural mill.

Obeyesekere acknowledged Geertz's influence, particularly when he introduces his idea of the "myth model," which is central to his psychoanalytic theory of culture. A myth model is a public blueprint for interpreting social behavior and events. Myth models are a public cache of symbolic resources that we use, often subconsciously, to shape our lives and to resolve psychic conflicts (e.g., unresolved guilt). An example of an American male myth model is Sylvester Stallone's Rocky. In this myth, Rocky, as Everyman, is given, by luck, a chance to "become somebody." Through his relations with a father figure (his trainer) and his newly found love (the "behind-every-successful-man-is-a-woman" theme), he is able to transform himself and to tap into his dormant potential. The public symbols woven together in Rocky's story are easy to read for all Americans (e.g., love, family, humility, "be all that you can be," upward mobility, and unpolished behavior equal genuine qualities).

Obeyesekere's notion of myth models coincides with the interpretivist task—he seeks to explain how Sri Lankan individuals use myth models to resolve psychic conflicts. The troubled individual transforms public symbols by psychically hammering them into "personal symbols." Obeyesekere refers to this personalizing process as "subjectification." Through subjectification, public symbols are subconsciously mapped onto repressed experiences. These experiences are then brought into the light of consciousness through "objectification," which refers to the public expression of those personal symbols by the individual.

The subjects of Obeyesekere's *Medusa's Hair* (1981) are men and women who enter ecstatic states of trance-possession, usually possessed by a god, a demon, or a deceased parent. There are religious contexts in Sri Lanka where this behavior is not only acceptable but rewarded. The successful synthesis of personal and public symbols permits individuals to "work out" psychic feelings of guilt in public settings without being stigmatized. Both processes are necessary to heal "madness." In fact, many of Obeyesekere's informants managed to transform trance-possession into both therapy and profession by acquiring a clientele that asks them to resolve problems thought to be caused by supernatural agents.

Obeyesekere's psychoanalytic approach differs significantly from Geertz's interpretivist position. Obeyeskere's goal is not only to interpret but also to explain behavior. His explanations rely on excavating the subconscious "grotto in the head," an approach Geertz would reject as a double dose of "psychologizing."

The distinction Obeyesekere makes between public and personal symbol systems implies that they must have different locations, with culture (i.e., public symbols) located in the public realm and personal symbols in the person. However, this distinction is largely a product of perception; public and personal symbols are active in two different arenas of psychic life: *on* the public stages where we traffic in symbols, and *in* the psychic arena, where our conscious thoughts, feelings, and unconscious impulses engage in a shadow dance.

The ambiguity inherent in Obeyesekere's analysis is that one is never sure where to place culture. On the one hand, Obeyesekere asserts that the "work of culture" is to reroute libidinal (repressed) energy into socially adaptive tasks; on the other hand, he shows how the individual takes cultural resources (particularly religious beliefs and rituals), internalizes them and then works with them to resolve personal and often traumatic and abusive experiences. It is easy to slide into saying that culture cures the patient, but it is the patient who is in this analogy the doctor, and culture is the medicine. Consequently, Obeyesekere slips into writing about public symbols as if they are exterior to the person, but they are not. The public symbols are really culturally conventionalized symbols, such as those shared by those Sri Lankans who participate and believe in the religious myth model he describes. Culture "works" because experience happens in the world, but it is, in Obeyesekere's analysis, our psyches that act on and make sense of those public and lived experiences.

Version 3: Culture Is Cognitively Distributed

Cognitive anthropologists have been the strongest advocates in anthropology of the proposition that culture is located in the head. This position holds that culture consists of the mental ordering of personal experiences into templates or *schemas* that are used to interpret sensory input and generate appropriate behaviors in any given situation. Cognitivists are perplexed about why people, especially other anthropologists, don't "get it." For example, while Claudia Strauss and Naomi Quinn were working on their book on cognitive theory, a colleague "suggested we leave out the word 'cognitive' if we wanted anybody to read it" (1997:9). They argue that Geertz's eloquent and sustained attacks on psychologizing and his equally eloquent proposal that symbols inhabit public and not mental spheres of life "contributed to the banishment not only of the cognitive anthropology of that time but all of psychologizing from mainstream American anthropology for a long time" (p. 254).

Strauss and Quinn, of course, reject Geertz's notion of culture as a system of public symbols that is not located in the human mind: "meanings cannot be abstract structures that are nowhere in particular (or a cloud hovering over Cincinnati, as a colleague of ours put it sarcastically)" (p. 19). Spiro also insisted that it is a big mistake to locate culture outside the individual, "cultural doctrines, ideas, values, and the like exist in the minds of social actors—where else *could* they exist?—to attempt to understand culture by ignoring the human mind is like attempting to understand *Hamlet* by ignoring the Prince of Denmark" (1987:161–162).

Geertz's argument—that cultural reality is to be found at the baseball park, among the rows of Muslims bent in worship on Friday afternoon, in the gridlock of city streets, and in the bustle of the marketplace—*feels* right and is certainly more exciting than saying, as cognitivists do, that culture consists of neurally configured mental representations of experience. But without a mind, without a memory to store, say, understandings and images of baseball, how do we know that what "they" are doing is "baseball"?

Schwartz (1978) provides a cognitive theory of culture and psychology grounded in the experiential rather than neural world. When Schwartz began his fieldwork on Manus, an Admiralty Island in Melanesia, he had assumed that culture was homogenous and that members of a culture act and think alike. The ethnographic strategy of the day (which he initially adopted) was to infer norms, values, and beliefs by observing regularities in behaviors and events. Behavior conformed to cultural standards and cultural standards were "out there," regulating behavior and thought. Ethnographies could be written that describe the culture and psychology of the people of Manus, the psychology being the internal crystallization of culture manifested in the personality types found among the people. The circularity was comforting.

After some months on Manus, Schwartz noticed much more variation in everything (beliefs, personalities, behaviors) than he had expected from his anthropological training. His option was either to sweep the inherent messiness of everyday life out of his ethnographic writing or to deal with it. Schwartz used three key concepts to develop his theory of the psychological basis of culture; these are "construct," "idioverse," and "distributive culture/cognition."

A construct is a mental representation of experiences and events including the evaluative and emotional particulars associated with those experiences or events (p. 425). An example would be going to the beach with your best friend. In your head you have a picture (the representational or formal aspect of the construct) of going to the beach, and with it you associate good feelings (the emotional connection) and also place a value on this activity, preferring it to "watching TV" in the set of possible "fun activities." Individuals attach an evaluative score to all constructs. The combination of the emotion associated with a construct and the evaluative score give a motivational force or "valence" to the construct. In this way, constructs motivate behavior and the higher the motivational valence of a construct, the more likely it will trigger behavior associated with the construct. For example, if "watching TV" has a lower motivational valence than "going to the beach" (we should hope so!), then the two friends are more likely to go to the beach (the actual behavior).

Constructs also vary in terms of specificity, articulation, and individual competence. For example, if you seldom go dancing, you may only be able to describe dancing as "slow" or "fast" or, in the absence of words, you may do a poor job imitating "dance." However, a dancing aficionado has very specific constructs about dancing and will be able, if not verbally to articulate it, then to demonstrate it. One's constructs are not mirror images of behaviors but are derivatives of experience that encode both past and possible, real and hypothetical behaviors and events. One can, for instance, imagine dancing like a flamenco dancer without being able to dance like one.

An idioverse is the sum of all one's constructs. An idioverse is each person's version of his or her culture; there is no public or superversion of culture. People may share the same construct in terms of cognition but vary in terms of emotional and evaluative associations. Thus, even though people share similar mental representations of a day at the beach, the image may appeal to some and not to others.

Schwartz states that idioverse and personality are one and the same; he uses the term "idioverse" because he considers idioverses to be the building blocks of culture and because the joining of culture *and* personality has a long and troubled history in anthropology. Culture is constructed out of individual versions of culture. By using the term "idioverse," Schwartz cleverly offers us an unfamiliar term, without historical baggage. However, by focusing on the idiosyncracies of idioverses, Schwartz is in danger of losing the core idea of culture—that it is shared—in favor of a view that shatters culture into a myriad of eccentric shards that are impossible to patch together.

Schwartz anticipates this problem and argues that people's constructs, their idioverses, overlap because they share similar life experiences. Our idioverses are not stockpiles of information but consist of experience-based information that is organized as a joined cognitive, emotional, and evaluative schema. The "union" of idioverses refers to the amount of "culture" shared by members of a group. Culture is distributed to the extent that the idioverses of members of a group necessarily overlap. Figure 1.2 illustrates the relationship between idioverses. The numbers 1, 2 and 3 represent the idioverses of individuals; the "+" designates their overlap. Schwartz defines culture as the "union" of all idioverse, including the completely idiosyncratic portions of an idioverse (p. 429). He holds that we cannot disqualify eccentric constructs from our definition of culture for two reasons. First, one person may hold unique knowledge that has vital significance to the members of that culture. (Schwartz gives the example of a tribal genealogy expert, but we might also think of any inventor, artist, explorer, or leader.) Second, the idiosyncratic portion of an idioverse represents a fund of potentialities that may lead to cultural change by entering the public domain, infiltrating other idioverses and spreading like a contagion. Idiosyncracies are the kindling that stoke cultural change.

In summary, cognitive anthropologists assume it to be obvious that culture is located in the mind of its members: no people, no culture. By reversing the figure-ground relationship between public and private, culture and psychology, as posited by Geertz and the superorganicists, cognitivists foreground (or "figure") the psychological and background (or "ground") the public nature of culture. Mental representations are derived from personal experiences and are constructed out of cognitive structure and content, emotional associations and an evaluative rating. Cognitive structure and content refer to the pictures (*gestalten*) in one's head. Emotional associations refer to the kinds of feelings evoked by a particular picture, and evaluative ratings refer to the preferential intensity associated with an emotion (i.e., rating a person's like or dislike for an emotion along a scale).

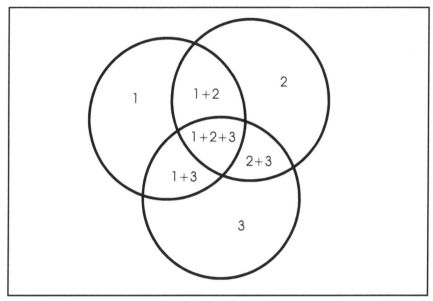

Figure 1.2. Three Idioverses and Their Intersects

REAL-WORLD IMPLICATIONS OF THE
"OUTSIDE/INSIDE" THEORIES OF CULTURE

Let me restate the possibilities: culture is either outside or inside the person. A sitting-on-the-fence position just compounds the problem because eventually one has to explain diversity *within* cultures, and to do so requires the use of psychological, conceptual tools. One also has to explain the diversity *between* cultures which requires the use of cultural tools. If culture is outside the person, we still have to figure out how humans "internalize" it. If culture is inside us, we have to figure out how it becomes shared or "externalized."

There are recorded instances of feral ("wild") children who were raised with minimal or seemingly no human contact. After a certain age, it is impossible for them to become linguistically competent and enculturated. The longer someone is literally outside of culture, the less "human" that person is, and at some pivotal point the potential to become fully human dies. Without culture we are "protohumans."

Those behaviors that are most biological came about because they are necessary for our species to survive—sexual intercourse, child rearing, food gathering—have always been shaped by, and expressed through, the force and medium of culture. Thus, to explain romantic love as having a biological function is fine as far as it goes, but it has little to do with the complexities, the ups and downs of those who are in the throes of love. Our cultural and psychological makeup are constrained by biological requirements, but in no way is this range either limited or reducible to biology. Without culture our biological requirements cannot be met. We are overwhelmingly cultural animals, and to theorize about the location of culture is to theorize about the nature of being human.

Implications of Outside Theories of Culture

If culture is outside, then it must still be caught by our perceptual nets, taken in, and mentally digested before we can behave in culturally appropriate ways. For Geertz, consciousness is, at best, an uninteresting dark room through which symbols briefly pass, are registered, and return back into the light of the public world. For the superorganicists, the proper metaphor for culture is the "container," or biosphere, with the members of the culture located inside.

Any outside metaphor of culture compels a theory of psychological and cultural homogeneity for the members of that culture. The outside theory of culture leads to the proposition that for any culture X there exists a member population $x_1, x_2 \ldots x_n$. By extension, for every culture (A, B, C . . .) there exist corresponding in-member populations.[9] Clearly, Hopi culture is composed of people who are members of that culture. Just as clearly, Trobrianders are members of Trobriand culture, Chinese of Chinese culture and so on. Figure 1.3 illustrates the outside theory of culture by representing two different cultures and their respective members.

The Figure 1.3 model of two cultures and their populations (represented by Xs and Ys, respectively) illustrates that any two individuals in culture "A" must be more similar to each other than they are to any member of culture "B." We could argue that the two cultures overlap. They can't significantly overlap, however, otherwise the term "culture" loses its distinctive meaning.

Suppose that culture "A" represents the United States and culture "B" India. Further, suppose that one X represents Donald Trump,

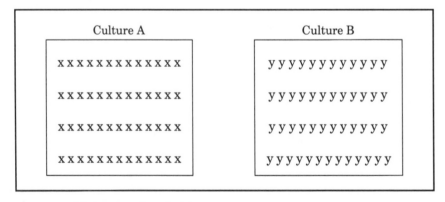

Figure 1.3. Model of an Outside Theory of Culture

another a fifty-five-year-old organic farmer and vegetarian in Oregon named Sheila Olsen, and one of the Ys represents a Hindu female multimillionaire from Calcutta named, let's say, Laxmi Chaudry. Outside theories of culture would imply that "the Donald" and Sheila Olsen are culturally more similar to each other than either is to Laxmi. But clearly there are experiences that Laxmi and Sheila share in common as women and perhaps as vegetarians and experiences that Laxmi and Donald share together as urban-dwelling multimillionaires.

An "outside" proponent might argue that Donald Trump and Sheila Jones are culturally similar but that social class distinguishes them. But each such appeal to explanations other than culture diminishes the explanatory power of culture by that much, until little is left. It might be argued that culture is a whole made out of parts such as class, religion, politics, economics, education, and so forth and that within-culture similarities refer to these aspects of culture and not to culture as a whole. This model of culture is problematic, for it reduces culture to a category label whose sole function is to signal, and sometimes stand for, those subsystems that shape the individual.

There are real costs to seeing culture as a homogeneous, bounded whole. Politically, such a view can be used to legitimate ignoring minority interests, enforcing assimilative cultural and educational policies and attending to those interests represented by the most visible and dominant members of that culture. Sheila Jones and all those who are significantly and noticeably different from the "typical" member of a culture (however defined) are perceived as outside the cultural mainstream; hence, statistically and otherwise deviant. Theories that define culture as unitary wholes cannot be used to endorse intracultural diversity. An outside theory of culture must focus on essential commonalities because it presumes that cultural forces (however defined) act on individuals and, in any given culture, these forces must be, by definition, the same.

Multicultural theories of culture endorse ethnic or subcultural diversity within the larger culture. The "salad bowl" analogy is commonly used as a metaphor for talking about a multiculturalist model of culture. The idea is that a salad with just lettuce is bland, and adding different types of foods makes the salad more interesting and tastier. The lesson, of course, is that diversity is good. But does the metaphor really promote cultural diversity? I think not, because, like a superorganic theory of culture, it implies the existence of *essential* differences between ethnic/subcultural groups: a carrot is a different kind of vegetable than a cucumber. The metaphor also conflates (that is, mixes) two levels of abstraction, by suggesting that taste is enhanced by adding different kinds of foodstuffs; but who is doing the tasting? A mix of carrots, lettuce and cucumbers enhances the taste of the salad, but the vegetables don't do the tasting. In fact, they don't interact with one another. Thus, the implicit message of the salad bowl metaphor is that ethnic/cultural groups are not only essentially different from one another but that they don't interact even if they are in close proximity to one another. This sort of multicultural "folk theory" is predicated on an "outside" theory of culture and is incompatible with what one presumes are the goals and ethos of advocates of multiculturalism.

More recently, Samuel Huntington, a political scientist at Harvard, argued that as a consequence of globalization there is a coming "clash of civilizations" (1993, 1996). He states that there are distinct national-cultural heritages and that current contemporary political movements rely on a rhetoric of cultural fundamentalism. Culture has replaced race as a means both to identify and mark in- as well as out-groups. Outside versions of culture saturate our everyday lives and discourses. Ulf Hannerz writes that,

> Suddenly people seem to agree with us anthropologists; culture is everywhere. Immigrants have it, business corporations have it, young people have it, women have it, even ordinary middle-aged men have it, all in their own versions. . . . We see advertising where products are extolled for "bed culture" and "ice cream culture," and something called "the cultural defense plea" is under debate in jurisprudence. (1996:30)

One of the anthropologist's jobs is, I believe, to ameliorate the gut feeling of essential differences invoked by popular and scholarly discourses of culture that rely exclusively on outside versions of culture. Christoph Brumann (1999:S12–S13) writes that discarding the term "culture" would "seriously hamper" anthropologists' "critical potential" to offer more complex versions of culture. The current misuse of the term does not imply that it should be discarded by those who know better, but rather, anthropologists should demonstrate (again and again) that there is diversity within cultures as well as between cultures and that much of what individuals perceive to be part of "their culture" (e.g., mom, baseball, and apple pie) is arbitrary and not necessarily shared by other members of their culture.

Outside versions alone cannot do this. Essential differences remain; ethnographic texts written to familiarize us with and sensitize us to other cultures only reinforce the essential isolation of each culture by portraying them as islands. We can only be "at home" in our own culture and, by this metaphor, are cultural aliens when we venture to any other island. As a folk theory and as a theory that generates public policies with regard to members of other cultures, the prevalent "outside" theory of culture is logically and psychologically flawed; it expects too much from us and does not address the problem of essentialism.

Implication of Inside Theories of Culture

The inside theory of culture postulates that any mentally sound person can learn the stuff of any culture given enough time and experience. No one person knows all of the culture, but people acquire competency in the stuff they need to learn—how to shop for food, open up a bank account, order at restaurants, and so forth. Culture is not a bounded whole; it consists of situated knowledge of different contexts and domains of experience. Culture is the problematical and contingent union of what is shared by people in specific contexts. It is problematic because we have to investigate what exactly is shared; and it is contingent, because we do not know how robust and how established the cultural practices associated with specific contexts are.

The superorganic theory of culture offers no explanation for individual differences, emphasizing only that cultures are homogeneous wholes. The interpretivist theory suggests that culture is locally situated in contexts rather than as a grand whole. Contexts are sites of practice where individuals read the movements and traffic of symbols. Still, those local, content-laden sites remain homogeneous wholes, like texts. An explanation of variation in social practices can only be explained by multiplying the number of cultural texts.

The inside theory presumes that culture has no meaningful boundary and is constructed from the inside out. For the inside theorists, culture is the object of analysis, that which needs to be explained; for the outside theorists, culture is the agent or tool of analysis, that which explains what we do and who we are.

In her article "Writing Against Culture," Abu-Lughod (1991) persuasively argues against any use of the concept of culture for two reasons: (1) ethnographies inevitably essentialize culture by "Othering" the people that are being written about (that is, emphasizing and exoticizing differences between the members of the culture under study and one's own culture); and (2) in doing so, we also inevitably perpetuate a relationship of domination and subordination that mirrors the colonial past. Abu Lughod and many other anthropologists have argued recently that there is no such thing as culture, that it is merely a designation that once identified a "people." They argue that to designate a "people" as a "culture" is not only harmful and unethical (Abu-Lughod's argument), but it is also logically faulty, as it confers agency to a label.

Even though it may be a totalizing or an artificial concept, there are, nevertheless, "times when we still need to be able to speak holistically of Japanese or Trobriand or Moroccan culture in the confidence that we are designating something real and differentially coherent" (Clifford 1988). The question is: how do we talk about both culture and what is shared among a people, without essentializing them? Recall Shore's statement about the absence of a locus for culture. We can still talk about culture by arguing that it is contingent and changes over time and across people and context. We can propose distributive models along the lines of Schwartz. Whatever we do, we should reject thinking of culture as analogous to a genotype, that is, as a fixed set of characteristics that we ascribe to a specific population and that are generationally reproduced. Like astronomers investigating the universe, anthropologists need to continue to investigate culture and to bring our new understandings to public attention.

Chapter Three

What (or Who)
Is the Self?

Know thyself!
—Socrates

Cogito ergo sum.
—René Descartes

I will forever remain a mystery to myself.
—Albert Camus

Self is the great Anti-Christ and Anti-God in the world.
—1680 use of *self*, *Oxford English Dictionary*, 1989[1]

A BRIEF HISTORY OF THE SELF

The first reported use of the word "self" was around the 1300s. It was used as a noun that packaged sin with the self. For example, the *Oxford English Dictionary* (1989, 14:906) offers the following as a typical use of the word "self" in the 1300s: "Oure awn self we sal deny, And follow oure lord god al-myghty." The above 1680 quote suggests that the association of self with sin has had a long history that continues into the present with terms such as "selfish," "self-indulgent," "self-serving" and "cult of the self" (Lasch 1979).

In 1694, in his *Essay Concerning Human Understanding*, the philosopher John Locke distanced the self from sin and religion by declaring that at our inner core was not an eternal soul but a perceiving self: it is, he wrote, "impossible for anyone to perceive without *perceiving* that he does perceive. . . . since consciousness always accompanies thinking, and it is that which makes everyone to be what he calls self, and thereby distinguishes himself from all other thinking beings, in this alone consists personal identity" (1994:449). For Locke, the "self" is the point of consciousness that interprets our experiences of the world. The self orchestrates our internal life and our "being in the world."

The problem with this commonsensical view is that, were it so, we could only access and study the self through introspection (through our own thoughts about our self!). Introspection is not a scientific method as it is impossible for two or more independent observers to study the same phenomenon (Gordon and Gergen 1968:1; Modell 1993:3). Introspection implies that each inward-looking explorer explores unique subterranean landscapes with different instruments. It is, therefore, impossible to generalize from introspection. Further, many researchers have shown that people's self-understandings and recollections are unreliable (see Nessier 1987 and Johnson and Sackett 1989). We are masters of self-deception, attributing more (or less) intelligence, humor, or some other quality to ourselves than is warranted. Introspection also denotes that we are consciously exploring the self. But with what are we exploring the self if not another self? How do we study *that* self. Like a fish in water, our self is always immersed in the pool or our own self-consciousness. The first step to the study of the self entails the step Locke made—to define the self in such a way that we can make it an object of study rather than the subject that studies. However, we need to develop better methods (and definitions!) for "inspecting" the self than introspection.

We will explore four major areas of contention in the study of the self: (1) Is there a single or are there multiple selves residing in our skin? (2) Is the self a necessary illusion? (3) Is there a new self, characterized as "fragmented," "divided," or "saturated," issued from postmodern, late-capitalist culture? (4) Does the concept of the self and/or the subjective experience of the self vary cross-culturally? Each of these questions holds up a different "looking glass" to the self and deserves individual treatment.[2]

THEORIES OF THE SELF AS MULTIPLE AND SINGULAR

The I-Me Distinction: From James to Goffman

William James (1892) was troubled by Locke's conception of an unchanging, perceiving self. He noted that the self is both a stable, coherent entity and, at the same time, malleable, changing over time and across contexts. To resolve the paradox of how an entity can be both stable and malleable, he proposed that the self consists of two functional subsystems—the "I" and the "Me." The "I"—also referred to as the "volitional self" or "Knower"—is the internal subject that formulates thoughts and actions. The I is like Locke's perceiver. The Me is the socially engaged self, the one we display to others. The Me mediates our relationship with the world and is the self that is apprehended by others. This distinction is grammatically underscored in James's choice of the subject pronoun "I" to stand for the perceiving singular "self" and the direct object "me" to stand for the self that is acted upon and must adaptively respond. For example, in the compound statement, "I went to school today and Johnny hit me," the I is not socially engaged, whereas the Me is realized and meaningful only in its social context.[3]

James thought of the I and Me distinction as a functional ensemble in which I establishes a historically continuous and unique self, while the Me is constantly adapting to new social and environmental circumstances. James posited that there is a Me for each significant other that one interacts with. To describe the dynamic between the I and Me he used the analogy of a herdsman/owner and his cattle herd. The Mes (or, in this case, "Moos") are the cows meandering about, and the herd owner (the I) is nominally in charge. While James was not entirely satisfied with this analogy,[4] his position was still Lockean in that he gave primacy to the unique and executive I and saw the various Mes as a sort of personal staff that deals with everyday social requirements.

John Ingham (1996) disagrees with James's I/Me division of the self and points out that for every knower there also has to be a self object, that is, a Me, to be known. I can't just be "angry" without also feeling that something bad has happened to Me. Once the I claims a particular emotional state, a Me must also be engaged to feel and express that state. Thus, Ingham argues that the I/Me aspects of the self are in a mutually constitutive and complementary relationship to each other rather than in a dichotomous relationship in which either one or the other self is operating independent of the other.

James M. Baldwin (1968[1897])—the evolutionary psychologist, not the novelist—Charles Cooley (1902), and George Herbert Mead (1968) saw the self as predominantly, if not exclusively, a social construct. In other words, the self is not inherently situated or in charge of consciousness, but develops out of personal experiences. Baldwin, a student of James, argued that the self consisted of an ego element and an alter element that are "interwoven" and form what he calls "the socius." Notice in the following passage by Baldwin how the importance of a unique self, or I, recedes:

> The development of the child's personality could not go on at all without the constant modification of his sense of himself by suggestions from others. So he himself, at every stage is really in part some one else, even in his own thought of himself. . . . He thinks of the other, the alter, as his *socius,* just as he thinks of himself as the other's *socius.* . . . In short, *the real self is the bipolar self, the social self, the socius.* (1968:165; italics in original)

For Baldwin, the socius "lives in" the person as a kind of introjected animus; at the same time, individuals "project" their socius out where it is introjected by significant others.[5] Obedience and accommodation to custom and tradition spread via this contagious process of projection and introjection.

This systemic reproduction and transmission of culture raises the question, "how does cultural change occur?" A second, perhaps more damaging, question is: "why are people different?" We have no difficulty recognizing that twins, despite their resemblances, are different individuals. By spotlighting the Me and diminishing the role of the I, Baldwin, Cooley, and Mead suggest that the self is a mere copy of cultural role templates. They cannot, therefore, explain either individual differences or social change.

George Herbert Mead (1968) recognized an I–Me contrast but acknowledged that the I has a role to play in the life of the self. The I is most obviously displayed by children, who have not yet been socialized to modify their behavior in the presence of others. Instead of muting their behavior in deference to others, children often trumpet their presence. The I is expressed in their uninhibited, unsocialized behaviors. Eventually, as children become cognizant of others, they internalize a "generalized other" who mentally shapes their behavior to suit the social occasion.

Mead used the analogy of a baseball game to describe the relationship of self to generalized other. The actions of a first baseman are incomprehensible if you study that position independent of all other positions. The role exists and has meaning only in the context of the game. Similarly, while the self may *seem* to be autonomous, it is not; like the first baseman, its goals, actions, and its raison d'etre are shaped by the social games it participates in. Mead explained that "the organism does not become an entity to itself except in a social context; it does not get into the environment except through the social process. There is no self unless there is the possibility of regarding it as an object to itself" (1968:148).

For Mead, the I or "ego element" is the biological baseline from which the social self develops, eventually "transcending" (Mead's word) the biological self. The Me-self emerges out of and is shaped through repetitive, regulated social practice. Our actions and our private thoughts reflect how we believe others perceive us. It is, in other words, the generalized other that makes up the Me of the self. We can experience the force of this insight in everyday life. For example, I swim just about every day. When someone starts to swim in the lane next to me, my swimming is affected, even when I try to ignore that person. It simply cannot be helped. The presence of others alters one's awareness of oneself and, consequently, one's behavior.

Mead's I, because it is biological, expresses itself in spontaneous and unpredictable ways. These intrusions of the I into the otherwise continual, predictable stream of Mes is the catalyst for individual difference and, perhaps, though not so explained by Mead, for social change.

Mead, like those before him, retains an idea of the self as a unified entity, but it is not an underlying, foundational I unity. Rather, it is the abbreviated unity of self in social contexts. The idea of a single historical coherent self is not a requirement in Mead's theory. In any event, that function is satisfied by his stripped-down version of James's I—the biological, affectively spontaneous (id-like) self. Mead's theory of the self opened the modern and postmodern gateway for claiming that there are multiple selves inside our skin.

In his book *The Presentation of Self in Everyday Life*, Erving Goffman (1959) described everyday behaviors and proceeded to microanalyze them with a razor sharp, cynical logic. He offers a novelistic excerpt of an Englishman named Preedy who prepares to go for a swim while vacationing in Spain. Let me quote just a bit to get a flavor of Goffman's mode of microanalysis.

> He took care to avoid catching anyone's eye. First of all, he had to make it clear to those potential companions of his holiday that they were of no concern to him whatsoever. He stared through them, around them, over them—eyes lost in space. . . . If by chance a ball was thrown his way, he looked surprised; then let a smile of amusement lighten his face (Kindly Preedy). . . . it was time to institute a little parade, the parade of the ideal Preedy. By devious handlings, he gave any who wanted to look a chance to see the title of his book— a Spanish translation of Homer. . . . The marriage of Preedy and the sea! There were alternative rituals. The first involved the stroll that turns into a run and a dive straight into the water. (1959:70)

Goffman refers to this sort of performative behavior as "impression management." For Goffman, life is literally a series of entrances and exits from microstages on which we play different roles with different scripts. As in the interpretivist approach, culture provides us with the stages, the scripts, and the "masks" or "personas" that we put on to perform our parts competently, even with panache. Some people are better at managing their impressions than others. Spies are experts at impression management. Indeed, Goffman's methods have been used to train spies.

For Goffman, the I has completely vanished; only stages, masks, and scripts remain. The question of a real or genuine self is a nonissue for Goffman; we simply do not know what is beneath the mask. Goffman writes that

> underneath their differences in culture, people everywhere are the same. If personas have a universal human nature, they themselves are not to be looked to for an explanation of it. One must look rather to the fact that societies everywhere, if they are to be societies, must mobilize their members as self-regulating participants in social encounters. (1959:231)

We have moved from Locke's "punctuated" and unique self to Goffman's dramaturgical theory of the masked, self-regulating self. The biological, stolid and perceiving I has been replaced by socially scripted Mes. The idea of multiple selves is the current prevalent view of the self. But there are those who are advocates for a single, undivided self. We turn to them now.

The Singular Self

Those who argue that the self is singular emphasize: (1) that the self is "embodied"; (2) the consistency of the self; (3) our commonsense notion that there is a true, private self and a false, public self; and (4) our seemingly intrinsic desire to achieve mastery over some task, like learning Russian or how to play the guitar. I will take each argument in turn.

The Embodied Self

Paul Rozin and A. Fallon (1987) in an experiment on "disgust" asked people to swallow their saliva; the subjects found this not to be a problem. They then asked people to spit into a clean drinking glass and swallow their spit; this was a problem. Why? Are they not equivalent actions? They conclude from their experiments that we think of our self as bounded by our body. Thus, the self is not just a Knower or a Me, but it is a phenomenal entity—a body, my body. That which is outside the body is not me; that which is inside is me. My spit when it exits my body loses its substantive identity as part of me and becomes generic spit—a substance we consider disgusting to ingest.

The Consistency of Self

The Me of James and Mead refers to the person in her social role. Ignored is the person as identified by her name. When someone calls my name, I become immediately attentive. My name identifies me as an individual apart from my various roles. This is apparent in that a personal name is fixed and does not change with status, context, or time. The "name identity" meets the criterion of consistency over time and space and is a unique personal, not a social, identity marker.

So far the argument for a single unified self uses commonsensical observations and experiments to show that the self consists of a mind (psyche) and a body (soma) that are seamlessly interconnected as one historical, localized self. But this argument is, thus far, limited to one of identifying the self as an entity composed of enduring qualities and linguistic signs. One can still not speak of the self as one can a Me, in terms of a specific role (e.g., teacher) with attendant behavioral attributes, values, and motives. The Me/multiple-self theorists could grant the unified, psyche-soma, identity a kind of conventionalized background status, irrelevant to the actual analysis of the self as a social actor.

Oliver Sacks writes (I don't remember where) that for autistic persons life "flows" through them "like a river." They lack, as it were, a dam to contain selectively the thoughts, dreams, and perceptions that flow through. With autism, he writes, there is no self there. Though perhaps, it is that there are no Mes there, only a master consciousness desiring nothing; and it is we who perceive Mes as evidence of a self.

In the case of multiple personality disorder (MPD), the body has too many independent selves residing inside its skin. As in the case portrayed in *The Three Faces of Eve* or *Dr. Jekyll and Mr. Hyde*, the presence of more than one self in one body is usually a terrifying condition that, if not treated, eventuates in tragedy. In their study of MPD, Nicholas Humphrey and Daniel C. Dennett (1991) found that it almost always afflicts individuals who were abused as children for long periods of time. By creating other selves, the child creates a boundary that protects his or her "actual" self. Akin to autism, the actual self "leaves" so that abuse is inflicted on the other self and, in this way, the primary self displaces the abuse and attendant suffering. The construction of another self, in this case, is a last desperate defense mechanism that protects the "real" self.

The True Self

The idea of an "actual," "true," or "genuine" self as opposed to a "false" self is the strongest argument I know for positing a single yet socially complex self. Eva Ilouz writes, "At the heart of contemporary Western culture is the division between the staged self, enacting itself in the public sphere, and the true self whose home is the private sphere of family, love, and emotions" (1997:91–92). Shakespeare offers ample evidence (e.g., Iago in *Othello*) that, as Ilouz suggests centuries later, the stage for the false self is the public arena, while its true motives are kept under wraps. The domain of the true, self is, or should be, the private arena.

Ilouz shows how modern lovers, particularly during courtship, withdraw from the social world and build "islands of privacy" in order to establish a "romantic utopia" designed for two. This utopia is built from mutual confession and through revealing to each other their true, innermost self. This true self, by definition, cannot be multiple. Like a diamond, the true self may be multifaceted, but each facet is composed of the same true self-substance.

Goffman's idea of many masks and personas underscores our common assessment that public selves are "phony." For those who propose a unitary model of the self, it is the I that is privileged and granted authenticity and the Me that is considered a necessary but false, at best, protective representation of the self. The true-false self theorists reverse the James Baldwin, Charles Horton Cooley, and George Mead I–Me hierarchy by privileging the I as the authentic representation of the self and derogating the Mes to their utilitarian function in the real world. For example, Donald W. Winnicott (1958), a private/unitary-self theorist, argues that the false self acts like a foot soldier (or soldiers): to serve and protect the true self from the social world.

For theorists of a singular true self (e.g., Harter 1997; McAdams 1997; Modell 1993; Winnicott 1958) the world is bifurcated into a private and a public realm, with the authentic self residing in the former and the false self in the latter. The false self is composed of adaptive pseudo-selves that mediate the authentic self's engagement with the public world.

Arnold Modell (1993) posits an evolutionary psychoanalytic argument for a unified self. Only a perception of oneself as unified permits an individual to imagine what might happen if he repeats his past actions in a given situation. By conceptualizing oneself as a unified self, humans can project the consequences of their actions (and those of others) to a future time, by recalling outcomes of similar actions in the past. Thus, by imaginatively shifting between past, present, and future, humans have freed themselves from the "tyranny" of the omnipresent present. This gives humans a great evolutionary advantage over all other species, for we are the only species that can mentally simulate and assess the probable (future) outcomes of various strategies and opt for the one that both satisfies our needs or wants and minimizes our risks.

Acquiring Mastery

Cultures not only provide incentives for individual to acquire skills that serve society, but Modell (1993) argues (citing Edelman 1987, 1992) that we feel an "intrinsic joy" when we achieve mastery over a skill: mastery makes us feel "stronger" and more "alive."[6] By virtue of achieving mastery over a culturally valued skill, the individual differentiates herself from her social group. Hence, the concept of a unified self distinct from others cannot be just a product of Western culture but must be a panhuman phenomenon, for in every culture there are individuals who are recognized as experts. For Modell, this constellation of factors—the desire to improve oneself, the intrinsic joy of acquiring mastery over a skill, and the capacity to match and evaluate past, present, and potentially future experiences—are evidence of the evolutionary development of a complex self system.

Unlike the true-false self theorists, Modell's theory does not require a dichotomy but rather a multileveled hierarchy in which the private self is both necessary and dominant because it fuels and organizes the self-system (1993). A key issue is that his model of a unitary self does not devalue the Me as representing a false self. In giving primacy to the biological basis of the self, Modell also extends the definition of self to include the body.

A problem with Modell's theory is the "and then a miracle occurs" explanation syndrome. When a motivation is intrinsic, then, like the soul, we have to take it on faith. But faith is not science. Modell proposes a scientific, evolutionary basis to the unitary self. The logic that there must be a unitary self, because memories have to be recognized as one's own, is persuasive. Positing an intrinsic motivation for feelings of mastery feels intuitively right, but we need empirical evidence that it *is* right and not just a crystallization of a cultural bias.

THE SELF AS A NECESSARY ILLUSION

Using quite different approaches, Katherine Ewing (1990) and I (1992), both anthropologists, and Dennett (1991), a philosopher in cognitive science, have come to similar conclusions concerning whether the self is multiple or singular. We three contend that the very notion of a self is a necessary illusion. The self "exists" as a mental representation or construct, a language game, a constellation of narratives that humans tell themselves; whatever it is, we agree, the self is not an actual thing. There is no self (or selves) enthroned somewhere in the head (or elsewhere).

Theorists who posit the existence of multiple or single selves are guilty of Alfred North Whitehead's (1927) "fallacy of misplaced concreteness"—that is, attributing substance or thingness to a concept.[7] Alchemizing thought into thing (i.e., reification) leads to thinking about the thought as if it really is a thing. For example, as discussed in the previous chapter, one can talk about the United States as if it were a self, made up of personality attributes and goals. This may not be bad politics and may be helpful when used sparingly. However, we know that the United States is not a living entity with a specific personality, and slipping into this form of anthropomorphism inevitably leads to simplifications that are logically false and often ethically and socially harmful, as was discussed at the conclusion of chapter 1.

I have argued that instead of a real self there is a "self symbol" (Hofstadter and Dennet 1981:200) that diffuses through consciousness so that memories, thoughts, feelings, and actions are symbolically framed as if they are anchored in and generated from a coherent and unitary self. Metaphorically, the self refers to a landscape of consciousness composed of "subselves" formed out of the store of personal experiences that are memorialized as networks of associated thoughts, feelings, and behaviors (de Munck 1992).

The self symbol is not a subself but, analogous to a radio, a transmitter of the sense of a genuine, solitary, integrated self to the subself that is, at the moment, "playing." The self symbol is the system of radio bands, the subselves are the radio bands themselves that comprise the system. Subselves acquire their own history over time and across contexts. The presence of a stimulus associated with any feeling, memory, behavior, or goal that is, in turn, associated with a particular subself can potentially activate that subself. The stronger the association, or the more associations there are, between a stimulus and the properties of a particular subself, the more likely that that subself will be activated. As stimuli change, so do subselves. For example, one may be feeling bored and tired while in class and suddenly energetic and happy afterwards.[8]

Certain subselves gain stability and robustness over time and are activated often, in the same way that some radio signals and stations are more powerful and popular than others. Many stimuli including very weak signals may activate these "robust" subselves. Hence these subselves are active across many contexts and remain relatively stable; consequently, the self becomes routinized and predictable to ourselves and others.

This model resolves the multiple/single debate by stating that the self is both multiple and singular, and it does not privilege one "type" of self over the other. But the model remains, just that, a castle built with words. We have no way of testing it. How can we describe a subself and the switching from one subself to another? How do we know that there is a diffuse self symbol? How do subselves develop? What happens at the moment of switching? Who or what does the switching? Ewing offers some insight into the switching process. Like myself, she argues that the notion of a whole, integrated, single self is an illusion. She writes,

> Individuals are continuously reconstituting themselves into new selves in response to internal and external stimuli. They construct these new selves from their available set of self-representations, which are based on cultural constructs. The particular developmental histories of these self-representations are shaped by the psychological processes of the individual. (1990:258)

In all cultures, people manage the "inconsistencies" between self-representations through "a universal semiotic process" (Ewing 1990:253). Ewing is advocating a new epistemology (that is a way of knowing or seeking to know) for studying the self by asserting that the ontology of the self (the "realness" that we attribute to the self) is grounded in language rather than in spirit-stuff or flesh and blood. When we describe the "self" (to ourselves and to others) we use words beaded into metaphors that serve to integrate separate elements into an organized holistic framework of self. For example, as one talks about one's desire for a full and happy life, one can talk about athletic, romantic, familial, political, leisure, and educational pursuits as if they were all part of the larger container: "a full and happy life." Each self-representation, however different, fits into this holistic idea of self through the medium of metaphor.

A self-representation is constructed of selected memories analogous, she writes, to a "curriculum vitae." Ewing posits the operation of a "contextual unconscious" that leads us to "forget" inconsistencies in our selves as we shift from context to context, self-representation to self-representation. This forgetting is critical in her analysis because it allows the self-representation activated in a particular context to experience itself as continuous, timeless, and whole, rather than fleeting and fragmented (1990:273). She states that the inconsistencies are not noticed and the individual experiences a single, integrated self as long as the "individual is able to maintain contextually appropriate self-representations in interactions with others" (1990:273).

Many of the same criticisms applied to my concept of the subself can be directed at Ewing; the two models are not so different. Ewing's contribution lies in her linkage of language use, particularly metaphor, with psychoanalytic concepts and cognitive processes in order to explain the simultaneity of multiple and singular selves. She argues that we are really multiple, fragmented selves but that we "forget" this and presume that our present self is, as long as it is performing competently, emotionally and cognitively invested with a sense of its own singularity and completeness.

Dennett (1991) provides the most extreme view of the "no-self" theory that he shares with Ewing and me. Dennett derides those who posit the existence of a singular self because he just does not believe that there are any selves located in the head at all. He questions, tongue in cheek, if there are multiple selves, precisely how many are there—2, 5, or 153? By asking such straightforward questions, he invokes the reification argument of "misplaced concreteness" against both multiple- and single-self theorists. He writes that for "real understanding to occur" we want "*someone in there* to validate the proceedings, to *witness* the events whose happening constitutes the understanding" (1991:322; his italics). But, he goes on, we can never mentally find that witness, that someone who is us, because introspection allows us to examine the content and process of thought but not the principles that frame those thoughts. We cannot access the "features" of the self-that-introspects, just as we do not have conscious access to those muscle and nerve activities that allow us to wink. We just do it (wink); similarly we just think us a self.

For Dennett, the self is both a narrative practice and pattern. As narrative practice, it is a linguistic construct by which we assign "I" to actions, thoughts, and feelings. Conversely, we also learn to identify certain sequences of behaviors, thoughts, and feelings with our self and assign a self "meta-tag" to those patterns. Bernard J. Baars (1997) uses simple text experiments to show that the brain works more efficiently when the symbols we read are organized into a discernible pattern. For example, let's take the following passage: "Mary had a little lamb." Time yourself and rate how difficult it was to read and understand that statement. Now read the same statement but in the following environment: "Mbatrqy mheawd la zlyiwtltplbe vloaxmibo." Again, "WELCOME Mary TO had THE a SOFT little PARADE lamb." In the latter two cases the mind works to extrapolate the pattern of words that it is "looking for." In the same way, our consciousness works to form coherent narratives from the incoming flow of perceptual input. Dennett (1991) refers to these narratives as "drafts" because they are minimal narratives, just good enough to make sense. They contain gaps that we don't notice. The draft may simply be comprised of "Mary" and "little lamb." The "had a" gets interjected when we need to say or sing it but is not required in our mental draft.

Dennett (1991) offers an experiment to show how we ignore gaps in perceptual input. Our parafoveal vision (the central area of the retina that allows us to make fine-grained visual distinctions) extends about three degrees off the center of our gaze. To make up for our poor peripheral vision our eyes "saccade," that is, jump, from object to object about four to five times a second. Now imagine yourself in a room in which the wallpaper consists of small squares with portraits of Marilyn Monroe. You are in the room for only two seconds. Almost instantaneously you will *know* that the wallpaper consists of thousands of replicas of Marilyn Monroe's portrait even though you will only have seen 20 or so at the most. The mind doesn't actually generate these thousands of portraits. Instead, in the absence of disconfirming information, it drafts a narrative that states that the wallpaper consists of Marilyn Monroe portraits.

In the same way, your mind convinces you that the self exists because *someone* must be authoring these narratives; there is no evidence to disconfirm that hypothesis. Multiple drafts, like notes on index cards, are sequenced into a coherent narrative, convincing you that they come from a single intelligent source. Dennett refers to this process of imagining drafts as sequenced into a coherent story as the "narrative center of gravity" (1991). Dennett chose "gravity" because gravity only *seems* to have a center. We don't really carry complete texts in our heads; we just carry the necessary segments of those texts to make it seem as if we have the full text. We don't "fill in" the other Marilyn Monroes; we just assume, in the absence of contrary evidence, that they are there, and our consciousness is supremely untroubled by this absence. The self exists because these narratives have coherence and must be authored by someone, so, in the absence of disconfirming narratives, we write in a self as the author of the narratives. We do this, I suggest, because as Baars (1997) points out, we are hard-wired to find patterns, and the self is the label we give to Locke's interior perceiver who recognizes not only the patterns of our perceptions but the process of searching for and constructing patterns out of perceptions. But unlike Locke, this time the interior perceiver is a linguistic sign rather than an actual central node of consciousness.

Dennett's analysis is based on three propositions: (1) Homo sapiens need and use language as spiders need and weave webs; (2) the brain scribbles drafts that consciously appear to form coherent narratives; and (3) these narratives are inferred to be produced by a single author—the self. In other words, the self is the conceptual by-product of loosely organized thought strings.

Summary

The shift to the self as a linguistic-cultural rather than a purely psychological (i.e., mental) construct makes the self accessible to direct study. The fundamental difference between these theories is a matter of the definitional lense used to frame or look at the self. Indeed, Ewing reminds us that "a single model of self or person is not adequate for describing how selves are experienced or represented in any culture" (1990:257).

In a review of studies of the self, Grace Harris argued that the terms *self, person* and *individual* be given nonoverlapping functional definitions: The term self refers to the uniquely psychological properties of the self. It is "the locus of experience" and consists of both I (self as subject) and Me (self as object) aspects of the self. Person identifies the human as an agent in (and of) society so that one's goals, attitudes and interactions are reflective of sociocultural norms and values. Individual refers to the biophysical characteristics used by a society to identify a person "as a single member of the human kind" (1989:601).

Harris's definitions are frequently cited but seldom, if ever, applied. Most contemporary scholars of the self reject "hard and fast definitions of these terms" (Skinner, Pach, and Holland 1998:14, fn2). In their introduction to their 1997 volume "Self and Identity: Fundamental Issues," Richard D. Ashmore and Lee Jussim write, "In this book, we have not imposed specific meanings on the terms *self* and *identity*. These words point to large, amorphous, and changing phenomena that defy hard and fast definitions" (p. 5). But researchers use definitions whether they acknowledge the fact or not. A serious problem with not defining what one means by self is that the meaning begins to shift with context and point of view, and the self (like culture) becomes, as perhaps it is, everything and nothing. Where an empiricist would recoil from nebulous definitions of key terms, postmodernists seem to be inspired by them. Indeed, ambiguity and the transitoriness of meaning are prevalent themes in postmodernist theory.

THE POSTMODERN SELF

In this section we will discuss the works of Robert Jay Lifton, a psychoanalyst; Kenneth Gergen, a sociologist; and Dorothy Holland, an anthropologist. Lifton and Gergen represent what is probably the most prevalent postmodern view of the self in Western society. They posit that the self is a reflection of the cultural zeitgeist (spirit of the times). The protean, fragmented, media- and information-saturated societies of the West produce, well . . . protean, fragmented, and saturated selves. Lifton and Gergen vacillate in thinking whether this a good or bad thing. Holland's work is influenced by Gergen, but her focus is on synthesizing life experiences with the discourses that people use to construct themselves and others in social contexts.

The Protean Self

Lifton (1993) coined the term "protean self" to describe the impact of low-grade chronic violences and the rapid breakdown of presumed ideological and structural stabilities on the psyches of people. "Protean" comes from the Greek God Proteus, who could change himself to suit any occasion. In the 1960s, Lifton lived in Japan for two and a half years and conducted research with survivors from the atomic bomb dropped in 1945 on Hiroshima. Lifton's more general concern was to study how our anticipation and experiences of death and dying affect how we live our lives and how we construct our sense of self. Lifton writes,

> I believe . . . our own death . . . is not entirely unimaginable but can be imagined only with a considerable degree of distance, blurring and denial; that we are not absolutely convinced of our own immortality but rather have a need to maintain a sense of immortality in the face of inevitable biological death; and that this need represents not only the inability of the individual unconscious to recognize the possibility of its own demise but also a compelling universal urge to maintain an inner sense of continuous symbolic relationship over time and space, to the various elements of life. (1993:253)

Lifton considers the post–World War II rise of chronic violence and massive dislocations of people from their homes and the dispersal of families around the globe to be the most significant factor affecting all of our lives, regardless of where we live. Consequently, the ability to retain a sense of "continuity" to community, culture, and, hence, self has been compromised. The creation of transient, ephemeral "communities" patched together by economic necessity has forced humans the world over to develop a flexible, rather than a stable, self. The "stranger communities" that most of us live in promote social apathy. Our search for life's meaning turns inward to the self and to personal relationships, rejecting the outside world that harbors terror and the unknown. I expect we are all familiar with this alienated, *Clockwork Orange–Mad Max* vision of contemporary life. For Lifton, we all live in a mongrelized, fragmented world where selves float on turbulent sociocultural waters like so much flotsam.

The protean self is a current psychological adaptation to turbulent, dislocating, and often violent global forces and conditions. However, Lifton infuses this globally bleak description of contemporary life with optimism. In contrast to the fixed self, the protean self continually renews itself, exploring new, "life-enhancing" possibilities. Authoritarian, racist, and ethnocentric ideologies rooted in essentialist assumptions are incompatible with the experiences and character of the protean self. Like Erving

Goffman, Lifton construes the self as infinitely malleable. But where Goffman emphasized the contrived and calculated nature of the protean self, Lifton heralds our ability to improvise as "life-enhancing."

The Saturated Self

In *The Saturated Self*, Gergen (1991) argues that "Under postmodern conditions, persons exist in a state of continuous construction and reconstruction; it is a world where anything goes that can be negotiated. Each reality of self gives way to a reflexive questioning, irony, and ultimately the playful probing of yet another reality. The center fails to hold" (1991:71).

Gergen's "postmodern conditions" are not centered on violence and tragedy, but on our everyday fragmented lives and the daily sensory overload that we are subject to. For example, there has been an exponential increase in the number of choices available for basic items such as tennis shoes, coffee, and lipstick colors. Confronted by these choices, we are pulled out of our selves and forced to make instantaneous decisions among too many choices that vary too little. Our relationship to coffee and tennis shoes has been altered, as is evident in the extended vocabulary we use to talk about these items. When we go out to have a cup of coffee with friends, we must disengage and redirect our attention on the options available, process the information, and make a selection. This kind of "information gangsterism," Gergen argues, robs us of a sense of centeredness.[9]

Even more than information overload, we are confronted by people overload. Daily we engage a wide range of people through different mediums of communication. Gergen depicts this stream of engagements as filling us up: the self becomes "socially saturated." To describe social saturation, Gergen begins his book with a wonderfully vivid passage of a day in his own life: a teacher at Swarthmore, he has returned from a conference in Europe, there is an "urgent fax" waiting for him when he arrives at school, students are waiting for his makeup office hours, his secretary gives him a list of all the calls he must return, there are e-mail correspondences, phone calls interrupt his meetings with students, a colleague is visiting—"by the morning's end I was drained." The afternoon is no different. This "intensifying saturation of the culture" necessitates a concomitant change in our sense of self. But what is the self?

The self is constructed via the medium of language; our vocabulary of the self establishes the ways we can think about, that is, understand the self. The self is not only created out of the medium of language but, for Gergen, the medium conceives the self. As language is the social system par excellence, so the self is a social system.[10] To legitimate and emphasize the privileged function of language as the stuff selves are made out of, he cites Ludwig Wittgenstein: "the limits of language . . . mean the limits of my world" (p. 5).

In other words, how you understand something is predicated on the vocabulary you have at your disposal to think about that thing. Gergen provides two interesting examples of this. The first concerns "love." He asks what would happen if we didn't have a word for love? We could use "lust" or "attraction," but these words don't convey what we mean by love. Consequently, he argues we would not be able to communicate the whole emotional complex of love to another. Nor, he argues, would we be able to feel love if we did not have a vocabulary to construct a discourse of love. In the second example, Gergen provides a list of mental health terms that refer to "characterizations of the self"—for example, bulimic, burned out, low self-esteem, self-alienated, anorexic, midlife crisis, and so on. He remarks that many of these are recently coined terms that refer to "mental deficits." He predicts that the growth of this deficit vocabulary, fueled in large part by mental health therapists, will lead only to an increase in the number of people diagnosed with these illnesses.

Gergen takes a strong culturally relativist position: different cultures, he argues, have different conceptions of the self. He strongly rejects the Western view that basic emotions, such as anger and love, or that aggression and the maternal instinct are universal, genetically based drives. An emotion is nothing more (nor less) than its expression; there are no deeper properties that underlie and shape discourses on emotions or self. The discourse is the emotion, is the self. Different cultures have different discourses. But what exactly is a discourse?

Discourses are *language games* (the rules and lexicon we use for speaking) associated with specific social interactions and situations. The game is both improvised and rule governed—like all games. A discourse is rule-governed in the sense that when we are chatting with friends over a cup of coffee, we do not mistake our friends for carpenters, bank clerks, or our parents. The vocabulary, register of speech, gestures, physical proximity are all, more or less, implicitly agreed upon without a discussion of the rules governing the social interaction. It is particularly important among friends to conceal the fact that there are rules that govern their social interactions. As in the television show *Seinfeld*, conversations switch from jokes to careers, from sex to politics, from everyday issues to life and death. The changes in conversation lead to different positionings of selves.

For Gergen, the self is predominantly a social construct. The self expresses itself and is apprehended by others with the linguistic/communicative resources at hand. In this sense, the self is a socially labile construct with the illusory stability of quicksand. If discourses are central to understanding Gergen's theory and the social constructivist position, we also have to ask where these discourses come from.

The "Self-in-action" Self

Dorothy Holland (and also Lutz, 1988) provides an answer to this question. She uses the metaphor of a bottle and liquid to describe the relationship between discourse and self: "These cultural discourses and their relationship to the self are not like the relation of the clothes to the body, but more like that of a bottle to the liquid it contains. Self-discourses and practices must be scrutinized, for they are clues to the contours of the bottle—the culture—that shapes the malleable self" (1997:165).

When culturally shaped discourses attain the status of official scripts, they provide ways of talking that legitimize and perpetuate inequalities and abuse. Powerful and shared cultural discourses on love and self are used to establish intimacy and create distance (Holland and Skinner 1987). A discourse based on American models of self-reliance and autonomy may used to justify "wanting space" in a relationship (Bellah et al. 1985). On the other hand, a discourse based on an American cultural model of romantic love may be used to justify wanting more intimacy. We paste and modify these cultural discourses to suit our own motives and speech style. Holland refers to these cultural discourses as "living tools" because they are what we use to think and act with. The self is a "site" where discourses "compete" for the right to represent the self. Discourses rise and fall, and are continually being shaped and re-shaped.

The experiential and strangely familiar world that anthropologists enter makes it nearly impossible to reduce the self of informants and friends to voices without bodies. Hence, Holland extends the social constructivist position to include the "self-in-action." She argues for an "embodied self" and offers this 1990 research example from Dorrine Kondo, a Japanese-American in a Tokyo market:

> As I glanced into the shiny metal surface of the butcher's display case, I noticed someone who looked terribly familiar: a typical young housewife, clad in slip-on sandals and the loose, cotton shift "home wear," a woman walking with a characteristically Japanese bend to the knees and sliding of the feet. Suddenly, I clutched the handle of the stroller to steady myself as a wave of dizziness washed over me, for I realized I had caught a glimpse of nothing less than my own reflection. (cited in Holland, 1997:178)

Kondo and Holland extend the concept of self to include the body *and* mind and explore how both are molded by cultural processes over time. Unlike the discursive self, which is always temporary and fluid, the embodied self is relatively stable and permanent. The embodied self adds a more historical and experiential perspective to the social constructivist position. The inclusion of the body opens up new fields of inquiry; for instance, we can now ask how cultural discourses shape and are expressed in bodily postures and gestures and how these bodily postures and movements are coordinated with speech. Though the self is culturally shaped, it is the individual who authors that self, who uses the living tools of culture to write the scenes and perform the actions that together make up the self.

Summary of Postmodern Approaches to the Self

Postmodernist and social constructivist theories of the self (I use the two terms interchangeably) question the existence of a "real self." They propose that what you see is exactly what you get—there is no homunculus, no Wizard of Oz or soul master pulling the strings behind the scenes. Everyday life typically consists of a stream of continuous encounters with different people in various contexts. In each of these encounters, at each of these social sites, the self builds up a self-history that is both improvised and ritualized—improvised because we never enter the same context twice, nor are we ever the exact same "self"; ritualized because we build up expectations about how to interact in various contexts and with various people. This improvised-ritualized self-in-practice is what Pierre Bourdieu (1977, 1991) refers to as *habitus*. Each individual expresses his or her habitus in speech, gestures and posture (but not in thought!). The way one sits in class, a hand under the chin, partially concealing the mouth is a habitus, a display of self. The self is inscribed in and expressed by the body. This surface fixation on the self is peculiarly postmodern and reveals the emphasis on fragmentation, contingency, and practice, for if one sees the self as habitus, as a stream of culturally variable discourses and practices, then there cannot be a notion of an internal and coherent self.

Kenneth Gergen's (1991) account of the "saturated self" (discussed previously) begins with a whiney riff about all the things that clutter up his day—day in and day out. His first insight is that there is no relief; and in that, there's a loss of self. The loss of self implies—his second insight—that there really is no executive self to begin with, only a vocabulary of the self. Daniel Dennett offers a hard-headed, scientific perspective of self and mind and concludes that it's all brainwork. But what human brains do best (or at least, most) is make internal and external talk. Dennett, the philosopher and embracer of positivist science, and Kenneth Gergen, the social constructivist and rejecter of the objectivist-scientific enterprise, meet and embrace at the junction of the illusory yapping self. Gergen and Dorothy Holland take a strong cultural relativist stance: discourses are constituted out of language and context, and selves are constituted out of discourses. Language is, as has been said, the social system par excellence, and culture is the human invention par excellence. Thus, we have ultimately built a circular loop: humans make culture that makes language that makes the self that makes us human.

This circularity is the ultimate problem of this line of reasoning. But the alternatives are that biology or God makes the self. Is there an essential foundational self? Is there a natural self-stuff that all humans possess? Or are selves purely cultural inventions? And, if they are cultural inventions, then are they universal? Why would all cultures have selves if selves were not in themselves essential? Social animals exist, after all, that do not need individual selves to create complex societies.

Aldous Huxley's *Island*, Ayn Rand's *Anthem*, and George Orwell's *1984* describe human societies where the self has been erased and the person is authored by the state. Each human functions more or less like a cyborg—a member of a social collectivity working for the common good. The next section addresses the question of whether every culture has a concept of self and how this concept varies cross-culturally.

DOES THE CONCEPT OF SELF VARY CROSS-CULTURALLY?

Amoebas must have a minimal sense of self because they must be able to distinguish themselves from things that are not them. Humans are more complex and therefore often act in ways that are more stupid than those of amoebas when it comes to understanding the boundary between self and not-self. Many Americans, for example, consider flag burning, a stranger tailgating their car on the freeway, or their child's inability to hit a baseball as an offense against themselves. Nonetheless, as the experiment with swallowing or drinking one's own saliva demonstrates, we take the self to be packaged inside us and be bounded by our skin, just like an amoeba. We assume that this is a fact of self universally shared by humans.

Second, most Americans, as Michael Lewis (1978) argued, perceive the self as a purposeful autonomous agent that desires control over his or her social environment. Lewis refers to this cultural model as the "self-as-central sensibility model of the American self." According to this model, we value self-reliance, individual achievement, willpower, and other displays of personal virtues and skills. But is this self-as-central sensibility model of the self found in all cultures? Geertz, speaking for most anthropologists (and most cross-cultural psychologists as well), answers as follows:[11]

> The Western conception of the person as a bounded, unique, more or less integrated motivational and cognitive universe, a dynamic center of awareness, emotion, judgement, and action organized into a distinctive whole and set contrastively both against other such wholes and against its social and natural background, is, however incorrigible it may seem to us, a rather peculiar idea within the context of the world's cultures. (1984:126)

Geertz must be aware of the writings of James, Cooley, Mead, and especially Goffman, all of whom have argued that the Western self is in fact multiple. There is also a problem with his criteria for defining the "person": what do criteria like "integrated motivational and cognitive universe" mean? One wonders if the converse—a disintegrated or nonintegrated motivational and cognitive universe—can possibly pertain to a functional human being anywhere. Are there stagnant noncenters of awareness?

The above quotation by Geertz is cited in many studies on the self; so it must be seen by many authors (including me) as making an important point. The quotation is intended to alert and to surprise, shaking the reader out of his or her cultural comfort zone. It also declares that our cultural construction of the "self-as-central" is cross-culturally rare and that elsewhere in the world the self is conceived of in significantly different ways. In this section I will (1) compare cultural relativist and cultural universalist approaches to the study of the self, (2) describe some ethnographic studies of the self in non-Western societies, and (3) summarize some recent cross-cultural studies on the self.

Cultural Relativist Theories of the Self

Cultural relativists are comparative in the minimalist, but important, sense that all anthropologists necessarily rely on their own "native" beliefs, values, and knowledge to work and live among people of another culture. What captures the anthropologist's attention is the differences; the more exotic those differences, the more they intrigue and the more they are in need of explanation. Similarly, the more exotic the culture appears to the anthropologist, the more exotic the anthropologist appears to the members of the culture and the more likely they are to modify their behavior around him or her, particularly if they perceive the anthropologist (as they usually do) as a person who possesses political and economic power.

"Reflexivity" refers to the anthropologist's reflections of the biases that shape his or her relationship and understanding of "the Other." "Reactivity" refers to the locals' reactions to the stranger in their midst. Both reactivity and reflexivity serve as double biases that affect fieldwork observations and results, particularly in the first stages of that work. Thus, one relativist criterion for studying the self in other cultures is to be reflexively aware of one's own subjective biases, in particular to recognize the cultural and political forces that condition one's own perceptions of the other (Whitaker 1996a:470–473). One's own cultural assumptions function as a springboard from which one jumps to the other culture's side and learns (or attempts to learn) the life-world from that emic—or indigenous—perspective. The strong reflexive view is that any ethnographic investigation is, in reality, a product of one's own cultural understandings and thus tells us more about ourselves than about the "real" other. If we claim that our studies are "investigative" and "objective," then they are arrogant and misleading at best and are a process of textually recolonizing the other at worst. Thus, a relativist account of the self must take reflexivity into account and recognize the limitations of any such studies.

A second criterion, central to the relativist position, is that cultures, selves, or any other complex concept cannot be reduced to a list of trait variables but must be studied holistically. A culture or a self is not equal to the sum of its parts, but each is an organized and complete pattern, a gestalt. Philip K. Bock (1999:49) uses the apt analogy that a culture is to its parts as a melody is to its notes. If one lists all the notes in a table or puts them all in a different order, then one loses the melody. One can also replace all the notes with different notes and retain the melody. In other words, culture cannot be reduced to its parts, and isolated trait lists do not reflect the cultural whole. Similarly, the self is not equivalent to its parts; one must take into account the relationship between "parts" and how the pattern of relationships constitute a whole in order to understand the self. Shweder and Bourne write that holists are "theoretically primed to contextualize objects and events, and theoretically disinclined to appraise things *in vacuo*, in the abstract" (1984:153, italics in original).

While the vast majority of anthropologists take cultural relativism for granted, they no longer presume that cultures are bounded wholes. Cultural relativists retain a holistic perspective by using a narrower theoretical lens and by focusing on context rather than culture. The self is situated *in* action and is not analyzed *out* of action (i.e., the SELF writ large).[12] The point is well taken. The self can now be ethnographically observed, and individuals can be asked questions about the self that are relevant to particular contexts. Cultural relativists reject grand (nomothetic) theory in favor of locally situated (ideographic) theory. The scaling down of theoretical ambition allows for greater focus and a more perspicuous rendering of life lived. Cultural relativists rely on obtaining "experience near" descriptions through informal conversations and participant observation of the "self-in-action."

Comparative Theories and Studies of the Self

A. Irving Hallowell (1950; 1955) was the first to argue that individuals live in and are part of a "culturally mediated behavioral environment." Hallowell wrote that what members of a society consider to be natural is, very likely, culturally constituted and definitely experienced *through* culture. If experiences are culturally mediated then, according to Hallowell, "self-consciousness, self-identification and reference, self-evaluation, self-stimulation, . . . [and] . . . self-control" must be universal attributes of the self (1950:169–170). Individuals are aware of themselves and others as actors in a social arena; they can evaluate their own behaviors as well as that of others, control their emotions when necessary, and be self-motivated to achieve goals. Hallowell insisted that the self must be reflexive (i.e., perceive itself) if it is to function in a culturally mediated environment. Hallowell proposed that the self is both a universal, psychobiological necessity and a cultural construct, thus synthesizing relativist and universalist positions. His ideas have greatly influenced the works of Ted Schwartz, Don Hollan and Mel Spiro (to name a few) as well as psychoevolutionary theorists.

Alan Howard (1985), Doug Hollan (1992), and Melford Spiro (1993) have argued that cultural relativists have exaggerated the claim of a "peculiar" Western concept of the self as unified and autonomous—as opposed to the non-Western self that Shweder and Bourne (1984:128) describe as "sociocentric organic." Howard rhetorically questions the claim that non-Westerners do not have a sense of a unique self by asking, "how do they deal with the corporeal reality of the body—the fact that it urinates and defecates and experiences hunger, thirst, and sexual urges?" (1985:414). This observation describes an empirical and embodied self, rather than a discourse-centered self. Hollan (1992) observes that the distinction between the cultural "concept of the self" and the "subjective experiences of the self" is seldom addressed by anthropologists (p. 284). He suggests that cultural relativist claims rest on discourses of the self— "cultures have different ways of conceptualizing and talking about the self" (p. 284)—rather than on how the self experiences the world.

Hollan criticizes discourse-centered/cultural-relativist theories of the self on the following grounds: (1) discourse-based models of culture are always generic or typical and leave out the "blooming, buzzing" confusion of our actual experiencing self; (2) such models serve as "premises" or guidelines for behavior and should not be confused with the actual behaviors themselves; and (3) discourse-based models "underplay" the influence of "psychobiological propensities" in shaping subjective experiences (Hollan 1992:285–286).

The universalist approach is a necessary corrective to the cultural relativist disposition, which views the self as solely culturally constructed and also conflates the conceptual with the experiential self. Nevertheless, as we are never going to have direct access to other people's self experiences, discourses on such experiences may be as close as we are ever going to get to studying primary experience. Both a relativist perspective attuned to noting differences *and* a universalist perspective attuned to finding similarities are needed to find out the ways selves vary or are similar cross-culturally.

Michelle Rosaldo's (1980) ethnography of the Ilongot tribal people of the Philippines was a landmark cultural relativist study of the self and emotions. She used rich ethnographic accounts to argue that emotions and, by extension, conceptions of the self are culturally constituted in context and are not biological essences that shape culture. The Ilongot have a mixed small-scale economy based on hunting, fishing and swidden cultivation. The Ilongot had also been headhunters. Killing was motivated by the arousal of an emotional complex referred to as *liget*, which is roughly translated as becoming suddenly and volcanically enraged. Ilongot conceptions of masculinity were based on the man's failure or success at taking a human head. The Ilongot explain that young men are made "heavy" by liget and have a "relentless zeal to take heads" (1980:63). The taking of a head is a "symbolic process" by which young men remove "certain burdens of life" such as insults or grief over a death. The victim is hacked until "you couldn't see its bones." The Ilongot men then celebrate by singing and dancing with unrestrained joy.

Rosaldo recorded songs, Ilongot discourses, and discussions that she had with the men in order to understand how liget is used to help Ilongot men understand "the significance of disturbing feats for daily interactions" (1980:27). Liget, she explains, is constructed out of public discourses that people access in order to label and justify their feelings. A man feels liget because that is the feeling he is supposed to have in that particular cultural context. Self and culture make each other up because a person appropriates a culturally constructed discourse to make sense of his feelings.

Unlike Westerners, the Ilongot, Rosaldo claims, do not have an "autonomous inner life" and therefore do not suffer either from repressed anger or guilt for head-hunting. Their emotional disposition also changes, for as men mature, liget gradually gives way to *beya*, which is knowledge and civility and is used to control liget. Emotions and the self are culturally constituted and therefore are incommensurate across cultures, given Rosaldo's strong relativist position.

Kondo, in her book *Crafting Selves* (1990), develops much the same argument. She refers to the Western concept of the self as the "anaphoric I," which is autonomous and bounded, moving across social contexts and landscapes and through time. The Japanese self, on the other hand, is always adapting to its context. Westerners perceive their private self as imbued with "real feelings" (p. 33) that transcend those artificial feelings of humans in their public role. For Westerners, society is perceived as "spatially and ontologically distinct from self" (p. 33). Her ethnography describes the multiplicity of working and informal social contexts that shape the Japanese sense of self as a relational rather than a private self. Kondo describes how images in the movies and activities in the workplace and neighborhood reinforce a sense of the self embedded in networks of relations, particularly hierarchical ones. Even in the privacy of her own flat she could not separate herself from society. Neighbors called and made assessments depending on whether she kept a clean house and woke early or late. In turn, the appraisal of the self as social rather than private leads to a greater sense of social responsibility and conformity and a desire to succeed as a member of a team rather than as an individual.

In her eloquent and superb ethnography *Veiled Sentiments,* of the Awlad 'Ali Bedouin women living in northern Egypt, Abu-Lughod (1986) describes how the women's sense of themselves and their behaviors change as they move from the public world into the intimate and inner world of the kitchen. In public contexts women veil themselves, control their emotions, and act modestly. The term for the feelings and expression of deference and modesty is *hasham.* Allusions to sexuality in any public forum will cause most women physical and emotional distress.

Veiling is an act of deference, but it is also symbolizes a woman's attempt to distance herself from and deny interest in anything that alludes to sex. Abu-Lughod describes an incident in which a divorced woman, in a room with the elder man of her lineage, veiled herself when the one-and-a-half-year-old daughter of the man crawled across the floor bare-bottomed (pp. 161–162). In public arenas, women's conceptions of self and expressions of self should adhere to the code of hasham. Abiding by the code of hasham is the only avenue by which women can acquire honor and prestige. Thus, they do not perceive themselves constrained by hasham; rather, they are self-motivated to act accordingly. In this way, the women themselves help to support their own subordination.

When among their female peers, however, these women act and view themselves very differently. In this context women laugh, sing, dance, and recite *ghinnawas*—poems that express their longings and sentiments, particularly those of unrequited love. Where public life involves filtering one's emotions through a medium of social censorship, the kitchen door provides entree into a much more emotionally ebullient realm of life. Ghinnawas are a "privileged discourse" that counterbalance, even refute, the dominant ideology represented by hasham.

Abu-Lughod does not, however, reduce the public self of Awlad 'Ali women to Goffman's "impression management," thus privileging the private self as "true" and the public self as "false." Both types of selves are equally valid and important to Awlad 'Ali women. Nor does she argue that emotions are pure cultural constructs, for sexual and romantic emotions are denied expression and repressed (psychological constructs) in public life, but are given voice in ghinnawas.

Abu-Lughod offers a cultural relativist description of the self in which culture is not the *only* determinant of emotions and the self. For Abu-Lughod, culture is the primary determinant of conceptions of the self, but to understand the emotional range of Bedouin women one must also take into account the biologically derived motivations, particularly sexual desire. Though she doesn't cite Freud, her concluding analysis is distinctly Freudian. She writes that "poetry may be so cherished by the Bedouins precisely because it allows people to express, and their intimates to appreciate, the profundity of that which must be overcome to conform to society's values" (1986:246). What is overcome is the repressiveness of the dominant public ideology. She writes that "vulnerability" and "deep attachments" (referring mostly to unrequited love and the cultural restraints on expressing deep emotions publicly) "are natural experiences that fall outside of culture." But what is outside of "culture" is the biological derivations of those "natural experiences." She goes on:

> Thinking in hydraulic terms, one might propose that what is excluded in forming a given cultural system erupts, if not in ordinary public discourse, then somewhere else—in the Bedouin case, in poetry. This "eruption" idea would imply that official ideology not only

cannot wholly determine the experiences of individuals living in a particular society but also cannot encompass the range of their experiences. (pp. 256–257)

Abu-Lughod comes to her Freudian analysis from, of all things, a social constructivist/cultural relativist perspective: the self and identity are expressed via cultural discourses. She relies on the concept of repression, not out of an a priori bias to use psychoanalytic variables for her analysis, but because her ethnographic data led her there. Her analysis is reminiscent of Modell's theory of the multilayered private self, while that of Rosaldo, Holland, and Lutz are theoretically influenced by Gergen. What I find exciting about this is that Abu-Lughod has, albeit unintentionally, shown that it is possible to synthesize successfully a constructivist/cultural relativist perspective with one that advocates psychic unity. Further, her ethnographic information led her to recognize that in the background, behind the closed kitchen door, lurks a private self that is "autonomous" (her word) and finds expression in intimate encounters backstage, removed from the public spotlight. This recognition of an autonomous self is important because it counters the reverse bias that often permeates the work of social constructivist/interpretivist-inspired ethnographies: that all other cultures have warmer, richer, more cooperative, and distinctly other types of selves than do Westerners.[13]

Comparative, Cross-Cultural Studies

Cross-cultural researchers usually do not rely on extended fieldwork to collect data. Instead, they rely on surveys or archival material to collect their data. The advantages of "experience far" (secondhand or survey data) over "experience near" data are that one can compare many cultures using the same survey instruments. The aim of cross-culturalist research is to test nomothetic theories, that is, theories that are intended to cast their explanatory net across the human species (no issues of reflexivity here!). The work of Harry C. Triandis, Karen and Ken Dion, and Hazel Rose Markus and Shinobu Kitayama are discussed below.

Triandis (1989) proposed that there are three dimensions of self, which he introduces as the most general types of selves available to all humans: the private self, where evaluations of the self are made in terms of a self-conception of a unique self; the public self, where assessments of the self are made with reference to an internalized "generalized other" (e.g., people, parents); and a collective self, where assessments of the self are made in terms of an internalized "reference group" (e.g., students, family) (p. 507). Triandis hypothesizes "that people sample these three kinds of selves with different probabilities, in different cultures, and that has specific consequences for social behavior" (p. 507). "Sampling" stipulates that individuals can choose from one of the three possible selves.

To compare sampling frequencies among these categories of selves cross-culturally, Triandis used the Twenty Sentences Completion Test, in which individuals write responses to the phrase "I am . . ." Responses that involve personal attributes ("lazy" or "bold") indicate that the private self was sampled; statements that signify a group (e.g., "Christian") reflect use of the collective self; and statements referring to a generalized other ("kind to people") indicate use of the public self. Geerz Hofstede (1980) applied this model and found a broad division between Euro-American culture(s) and the rest of the world. Subjects from the United States and Europe sampled the private self most frequently, and Asians, Africans and South American respondents sampled the collective and public selves most frequently.

Triandis's study was slightly more complicated; he differentiated cultures on the basis of complexity (using measures such as writing, levels of social stratification, presence of money, population densities, etc.). He hypothesized that the more complex a culture, the more "in-groups" a person belongs to and the less committed (or invested) the individual is to any one of those in-groups. Therefore, he predicted that members of complex societies will most frequently sample the private self.

The correlation turned out to be curvilinear—both members of simple foraging societies like the Dobu/'Ju of the Kalahari Desert and of complex societies like the United States sampled the private self most frequently. People from mid-range horticultural societies most frequently sampled the public and collective selves. The collective self was most often selected when behaviors are sanctioned by the norms and values of an in-group. In collectivist societies with rigid norms and rules governing behavior, individuals sample the public self most frequently. Triandis concludes that "a major determinant of social behavior is the kind of self that operates in the particular cultures" (1989:515).

This is a fascinating study because it distinguishes between two kinds of "Mes": those which identify with a generalized other and those which identify with a group. In addition, Triandis investigated relationships between cultural factors—cultural complexity, cultures with tight and loose norms, and socialization factors (not discussed above)—and kinds of selves. Triandis cut through a theoretical and methodological Gordian knot by operationally defining the self as a scalable variable. Interestingly, Triandis took his study still one step further by wondering what would happen if we compared the self along a rural–urban continuum within a culture. In so doing, he adopted an "inside-structuralist" rather than "outside" view of culture, by hypothesizing that differences in self-conceptions are a function of community size (remember this is Simmel's [1950] structural variable) rather than of cultural differences (where the researcher assumes that cultures are homogenous wholes). In his study of rural–urban differences, Triandis found that urbanites sampled the private self more frequently than people living in rural communities and that the latter sampled public and collective self-traits more frequently than did urbanites. In other words, many anthropologists may be guilty of exoticizing the Other when they look only for differences in self-conceptions between rather than within national cultures.

Dion and Dion (1996) used a similar methodology but refined it somewhat. They argued that both cultures and individuals can be categorized as collectivist or individualistic and that individualistic individuals can dwell in collectivist societies and vice versa. Thus, they attempted to account for differences within, as well as between, cultures by developing a two-by-two table of possibilities: psychological individualism, cultural individualism, psychological collectivism, and cultural individualism. Psychological individualism and collectivism refer to those attitudes at a personal level independent of the cultural characterization.

They hypothesized that cultures and individuals that score high on individual traits would value romantic love as a basis for marriage, whereas cultures and individuals that score high on collective traits would be less likely to value romantic love as a basis for marriage. Not surprisingly, Western subjects scored high on cultural individualism and subjects from Eastern cultures scored high on collectivism. Collectivism at the psychological level "facilitates intimacy within the in-group," particularly with family. Individuals who scored high on psychological individualism, regardless of cultural membership, scored high on enjoying love but seemed to care less for their partner and valued marriage less than did the collectively oriented individuals.

Markus and Kitayama's 1991 article "Culture and the Self: Implications for Cognition, Emotion, and Motivation" threads their own comparative study of the self in Japan and the United States with a general survey of culture and self studies. Using different terms, but meaning fundamentally the same thing as Triandis and the Dions, Markus and Kitayama argue that there are two universal "construals of the self": an independent and an interdependent self. The independent view is found in Euro-American cultures, and the interdependent one is "characteristic" of most cultures elsewhere. They argue that "interdependent selves" are typically found in cultures where people are pervasively attentive to how others perceive them and shape their behavior accordingly. "Independent selves," on the contrary, perceive themselves as autonomous, bounded, and find their feelings, goals, and actions to be centrally meaningful.

Markus and Kitayama demonstrate the differences between the two types of selves with two diagrams. In the "independent self" diagram, the self is drawn as a solid lined circle with x's inside that refer to various images of self; other selves such as *friends, father, worker, siblings* are represented as smaller circles located around the self circle with some touching, but none overlapping, the self circle: self and others are separate. The diagram for the interdependent self uses a broken-lined circle to represent the social porousness of the self. It should be noted that the x's inside the broken-lined circle of the interdependent model refer only to social others and not to various images of the self. Other circles, representing various significant others, overlap the self circle. In other words, the independent self's boundary is solid, coterminous with his/her skin and the interdependent self's boundary is "porous," extending and interpenetrating the self space of others: self and others are interconnected.

These differences have important implications for how individuals think, feel, and act. Markus and Kitayama (1991) conclude that the interdependent self's thoughts, feelings, and actions are guided by their "self-in-relation to specific others in particular contexts" (p. 227). The independent self perceives him/herself as an intentional agent "who is conscious of being in control over the surrounding situation and the need to express one's own thoughts, feelings, and actions to others . . . such actions of standing out are often intrinsically rewarding because they elicit pleasant, ego-focused emotions (e.g., pride) and also reduce unpleasant ones (e.g., frustration)" (p. 246).

Unfortunately, I know very few students, working poor, or middle-class employees who feel as if they are in control of their surroundings; nor do I know many people who desire to "stand out." Most shudder from the very idea. I also don't believe that Westerners consider themselves bounded autonomous wholes all the time nor that everyone else sees themselves as porous, extending into others. Poppycock! As noted at the beginning of this section, even amoebas recognize their boundedness. Ulrich Neisser (1967) noted that it is ecologically necessary for humans to recognize themselves as bounded wholes. The description of non-Westerners, particularly the Japanese, as having interdependent porous overlapping selves is faulty as a metaphor, for it implies that the boundedness of Westerners is to be read literally while the porousness of the Eastern self is to be read figuratively.

Metaphorically, Westerners are also pretty porous. For example, romantic love is prototypically perceived as a coming together of two halves to make a complete one (Singer 1994). Americans also consider themselves as part of a team; corporate culture and our institutions depend on cultivating team spirit. We even metaphorically portray ourselves as things, as in, "I turned the corner too fast and hit my brakes too hard and turned over."

SUMMARY

No doubt the cross-cultural studies cited above are important and have illuminated some significant differences between Euro-American/Western cultures and non–Euro-American cultures. Certainly there are cultures that, in the main, are more individualistic and others that are collectivist. But we are in danger of dichotomizing and reifying cultures so that these are the only two alternatives. Cultures and individuals must, like species, express "hybrid vigor" if they are to survive and thrive over time. The social constructivist warning that selves act and reconstruct themselves in context should be heeded. Collectivism and individualism, like independency and interdependency, are cultural narratives, stories, that we use to frame our perceptions of and our actions in the world.

Gregory Bateson (1972) noted that identical actions can be interpreted as fighting or as playing, depending on how we frame those actions. A "frame" is not the same as a "self," but it is a "living tool" that the self has access to. I would argue that the various aspects of the self described above are not really "selves" but are cultural stories that we use to frame our actions in terms of emotions, motivations, interdependency, or independency. For every context, cultures offer various stories with different outcomes, more or less popular, and the "self" chooses among these multiple stories—Dennett's (1991) "multiple drafts"—to act in the world. Cross-cultural studies are important for examining global cultural narratives of selves.

Much more work will have to be done before we can adequately link personal, contextualized narratives of the self with the decontextualized, abbreviated narratives of cross-cultural studies. What both cross-cultural and cultural relativist approaches show is that there are distinctive and broad pan-cultural conceptualizations of the self; that these conceptualizations are thus far understood dichotomously as designating either an independent or an interdependent kind of self; and that cultural conceptions of the self impact on the way people cognize and act in the world.

The theoretical approaches taken to conduct cross-cultural research on the self tend to rely on "outside" theories of culture that presume cultures are agentive entities (either structural or symbolic) that then produce psychological differences between (in this case) Euro-American culture and all other cultures. Inside theories could offer a more complex and more accurate view of conceptions of self by looking at how individual experiences shape both subjective experiences and conceptions of the self and how conceptions of the self may (or may not) vary depending on context. Such studies need not be culturally relativistic but investigate, as Holland (1997) suggests, commonalities in social practices across individuals and groups of varying scales. Where we find individuals who share similar clusters of experiences, we should find similar conceptions of selves. Such studies would not assume, as do "outside" perspectives, that there is but one configuration of self per culture. Though the study of the self is still in its nascent stage, I think that it is central to our understanding of what culture is and how we humans make and communicate meaning.

Chapter Four

What Is Meaning?

Concepts without percepts are empty; percepts without concepts are blind.

—Immanuel Kant

Like the notion of culture itself, the idea of "meaning" is at once intuitively obvious and frustratingly difficult to pin down.

—Bradd Shore

Our experience of reality is not what is in our world; it is what we think is in our world. What we think is out there is shaped by what we expect to be out there and what we believe cannot possibly be out there.

—Ed Hutchins

Before we get into the thick of things, I want to introduce some of the problems and issues concerning meaning through a few examples. These problems have to do with pattern recognition, levels of abstraction (or specificity), and "slippability."[1]

Think of all the ways you can write an "a" and still have people recognize it as an "a." You can twist and add, subtract, bend, curl, straighten, fold, and mangle that "a," and still folks will be able to squint and say, "Say, isn't that an 'a'?" There are many odd "a" shapes that people will recognize as an "a" even if they haven't seen that shape before.

How do we recognize the intrinsic "a-ness" of these shapes? Is there, stored in the head, a list of all the possible types of "a's" that can be made? What unconscious algorithm (i.e., logical procedure) do we use to assess the "a-ness" of, say, "α"? Certainly we have to have some preconception—that is, a mental representation—of what an "a" looks like and then use some sort of algorithm to determine whether that doodle is, or is not, an "a." Luckily, there doesn't have to be a one-to-one correspondence between the canonical shape of an "a" stored in your memory and the perceived "a." But there has to be some "family resemblance" between the two that allows you to identify the perceived squiggle as an "a" rather than an "o."

Questions over mental representations (and what to call them) and their relationship to "reality" become more complicated when we move up a level of abstraction. Suppose you had to predict what letter goes in the missing place in the following word, "sw-n?" Chances are that you will say "a" almost immediately. But if you unpack your reasoning or slow it down, it must have gone something like this: first you say to yourself, "It can't be a consonant." Then you try putting in all the vowels in the English alphabet, probably starting with "a" because you just know an "a" works to make the word "swan." Next, you will probably check out all the other vowels just in case. Some of the vowels almost make sense: "i" for example, but the "n" blows it; "swen" sounds vaguely Swedish; "swyn" seems phonetically like "swine."

Each of these various attempts to *figure out* what letter "fits" involves deciphering perceptual data and turning it over in your mind to make it "meaningful." The domain of meaning has moved up one level, from letters to words. As a consequence, we rely on a different search procedure for recognizing word patterns than for letter patterns. This kind of observation led to the idea that the brain organizes meanings in independent compartments at different levels of abstraction, because, as we see, meaning systems have different functions (Hirschfield and Gelman 1994; Sperber 1996). This is not unlike daily life activities, such as eating breakfast, teaching a class, and socializing, as these can be seen as modular (that is, self-contained) activity domains, with separate properties. These activities occur at an observable, phenomenological, level of meaning, whereas the beating of your heart and the neural transmissions of the brain occur at a "lower," unconscious level. Thus, there are many levels of empirical reality that can only be perceived either by changing one's conceptual lenses or with the aid of technological "eyes." For instance, the life cycle can be considered part of an evolutionary process that we are, largely, unaware of until we look at it from a distance. In other words, meaning systems are not only "modular" at the observable level but are also organized into and differentiated by hierarchical levels of abstraction as well.

The art of making meaning involves the creation of flexible feedback loops between concepts (our idea of what an "a" looks like) and perceptions (our processing of visual input). Thinking requires a marriage between concept and percept—divorce drains each of meaning. I have emphasized this point because it is central to figuring out how humans make, communicate, and share meanings. Without a common experiential baseline (or platform) meaningful communication would be impossible.

Meaning acquires its plasticity—its looseness—through the many potential associative links to various memories triggered by our experiences. For example, the concept "having fun" is associated with lots of different activities: eating good food, sitting and chatting with friends, dancing, or doing nothing at all. When one is 'having fun," one doesn't need to consciously reflect on it. "Having fun" is associated with memories of activities one has identified as fun kinds of activities. Dennett (1991) might point out that the memories don't need to be tapped; it is enough to "know" that they "exist." In other words, meaning depends on memory.

In addition, meaning involves a *self-monitor*—"a complex internal self-model"—that "allows . . . the system an enormous degree of self-control and open-endedness" (Hofstadter 1995:311). The self-monitor gives direction to mental processes of linking past and present and evaluating whether one is having fun. Without a "self-monitor" there is no way to evaluate whether or not "*I* am the one who is having fun."

Much of our conscious meaning emerges from unconscious processes. This is evident in word slips, such as the other day when my neighbor Jim asked if I had seen his swim flippers and I said, defensively, "Nope, I haven't seen your flimmers." A more interesting example of word slips is that instead of saying "a monkey's uncle" one says "an unkey's muncle" (from Jackendoff 1992:92). Three things are fascinating about this particular slip: first, the changing of the article "a" to the grammatically correct article "an"; second, though it is a slip of the tongue, we would never make a slip such as "onkey's lmunce"; and third, the change from "a" to "an" was done *before* the error occurred. Our unconscious mysteriously applies the appropriate grammatical and phonological rules to speech slips before they are uttered.

I conclude this introduction by reiterating the main issues that will be discussed in this chapter: meaning is constructed through the interaction of unconscious and conscious mental processes; meaning consists of the interaction between mental representations and our perceptions of real-world phenomena; meaning is monitored and directed by the "self"; meaning consists of modular domains hierarchically organized at different levels of abstraction; making meaning is a creative act; and, to paraphrase Dennett (1991), "meaning means to have a point of view."

The remainder of this chapter will follow the development of cognitive and symbolic approaches to the study of meaning and will be organized as follows: early ethnoscience approaches to meaning; prototypes and levels of categorization; schemas and cultural models; narrative models of meaning; and connectionist and analogical approaches to meaning. A brief note: the terms "ethnoscience" and "cognitive anthropology" are used interchangeably.

EARLY ETHNOSCIENCE APPROACHES TO MEANING

Goodenough and Psychological Reality

Ward Goodenough and Noam Chomsky provided the blueprint early cognitive anthropologists used for mapping the mind. Goodenough (1956:167) declared that the goal of anthropology was to describe what one needs to know in order to act as a typical member of a society. The implications of this directive are mind-boggling. Implied first is that culture consists of contexts and rules that govern behavior in those contexts, and second is that the "job" of the anthropologist is to make those rules explicit so that if a non-native followed them, she could not be distinguished from a typical native. Suddenly the ethnographic task was to zoom in on the minimal significant units of behavior rather than large sweeping observations. Consequently, early ethnoscience research seems pitched at such a microlevel of culture that the findings were often unfairly criticized as "much ado about nothing." The second major implication of Goodenough's dictum is that culture was taken out of the public arena and moved to the mind. The ethnographer's task becomes to describe culture *not* in terms of the behaviors themselves but the rules and mental images that produce behaviors and interpretations of behaviors.

Socialization is, after all, about children learning the rules for behaviors appropriate to specific contexts through trial and error. Eventually, they internalize these rules and apply them "without thinking," like raising one's hand to ask a question in class. Christina Toren (1993) provides a wonderful example of this; she shows how young Fijian children see individuals seated at a kava drinking ceremony as individuals, and as children grow older they gradually learn to see the seating arrangements as symbolizing the social hierarchy of the community. Eventually, seating arrangements are perceived as a configuration of statuses and roles rather than as a motley collection of individuals known only in terms of their relationship to ego. In other words, how one sees the world depends on what one knows of it.

The goal of these early pioneers of cognitive anthropology was nothing less than to "discover" the *psychological reality* that lay below the surface of everyday life.[2] The "new" methods of ethnoscience were said to reveal "what words mean to the people who use them" (Wallace 1969:397). Stephen A. Tyler in his introduction to the volume *Cognitive Anthropology* captured the excitement of the times:

> Cognitive anthropology constitutes a new theoretical orientation. It focuses on *discovering* how different peoples organize and use their culture. This is not so much a search for some generalized unit of behavioral analysis as it is an attempt to understand the *organiz-*

ing principles underlying behavior. It is assumed that each people has a unique system for perceiving and organizing material phenomena—things, events, behavior and emotions . . . . The object of study is not these material phenomena themselves, but the way they are organized in the minds of men. Cultures then are not material phenomena; they are cognitive organizations of material phenomena. (1969:3; italics in original)

But how were these "organizing principles" to be discovered? Tyler answers that "Naming is seen as one of the chief methods for imposing order on perception" (p. 6). Culture was not only moved to the mind, but it was to be studied through language, the social system we use for classifying things.

Chomsky's Innatist View of Language: Deep and Surface Structures

This move by anthropologists to weave culture, mind, and language together was greatly influenced by Noam Chomsky's (1986) theory of a transformational, generative grammar. Briefly, Chomsky made the following observations:

- Language is infinite: there is no end to the number of statements we can make.

- Language is complex: we learn to apply phonological, grammatical and semantic rules seamlessly and jointly without consciously thinking about them (most of the time).

- We know more than we can possibly acquire by rote learning alone.

- There are things in the world that we have never seen, experienced, or learned about, and yet we know how to classify and make some sense of them. (For example, in the statement—"Riri yakka snorted fire and devoured an entire army of men,"—what is Riri yakka?)

From these observations Chomsky derived two important conclusions:

1. There must be some underlying set of finite formal operations that we systematically apply to generate and comprehend language use.

2. Languages differ in sound, syntax, and vocabulary, but they are all products of the same innate language acquisition device (L.A.D.). All languages must therefore share the same fundamental deep structures and formal operations. There must be a Universal Phonology (based on the sounds we can utter and discriminate); a Universal Grammar (rules we use to sequence words into intelligible strings such as sentences.); and a Universal Semantics (knowledge and mental operations we use to convey and decipher speech or texts).

Chomsky's locus of study was syntax. He demonstrated that the deep syntactical structure of a word string does not simply, indeed *cannot,* mirror the surface structure because the latter is potentially infinite, while deep structure must be finite (it is located in the brain). That different deep structures alter the meaning of the same surface structural statement is made clear by the famous example "they are baking potatoes." In the deep structure, parsing "baking" as a verb or as an adjective alters the surface meaning of the statement. The deep structure consists of the syntactical rules by which nouns, verbs, and modifiers are ordered into meaningful statements. Chomsky's findings inspired much of the early (and present-day) research in human cognition. Chomsky's distinction between deep and surface structure implies that cross-cultural variations in behaviors and language conceal fundamental, underlying, psychological similarities that can be discovered only by investigating the deep structures in the mind that produce behaviors, including speech.

TAXONOMIES, PARADIGMS, AND MARKING HIERARCHIES: THREE UNIVERSAL COGNITIVE STRUCTURES

Three mental representations "discovered" and described by early ethnoscientists were taxonomies, paradigms, and marking hierarchies (the latter is the least researched). All humans use these cognitive structures to house and make meaning; these structures have a psychological reality as "natural" mental forms, which we use to organize and store information. The information housed in these structures is limited to specific *semantic domains.* A semantic domain is a coherent, "conceptual" area of meaning, usually marked by a category or class label. For example, "color" is a semantic domain that refers to all colors; the color "cornflower blue" would be an "item" in that domain. Cognitive structures *structure* the items of a semantic domain, and "meaning" is "discovered" by an analysis of that structure.

Taxonomies

Taxonomies are elicited by systematically asking informants the question "is *X* a kind of *Y?*" For example, one can ask, "is *X* a kind of mammal?" Taxonomies are structured as *inclusive* hierarchies, with the top level of the hierarchy referring to the category label of that semantic domain (e.g., "color") and the lowest level, the most concrete items in that domain (e.g., "cornflower blue"). "Inclusive" means that the lower level item (*X*) is a "kind of" *Y.* The aim of a taxonomic analysis of a semantic domain is to discover (1) the levels of inclusion and (2) the number and kinds of contrasting items located at each level. Table 3.1 shows a simple and, of course, partial taxonomy of colors.

What Is Meaning?   **67**

Table 3.1
Abbreviated Taxonomy of Colors

COLORS					
RED		GREEN		BLUE	
Maroon	Blood red	Emerald	Pale green	Azure	Cornflower blue

What meanings about "color" can be gleaned from this taxonomic structure? The uppermost level, also called the "unique beginner," consists of the label for that semantic domain or category. "Colors" is an abstract term that does not bring to mind any specific color but refers to all colors. Similarly, as we go up from "cat" and 'dog" to "mammals" and then to "animals," the life forms become more abstract until they cease to have a visualizable shape and consist predominantly of criterial features (e.g., warm-blooded, backbone).

The "red," "green," and "blue" level is called "the basic level." Basic level color labels are visualizable as distinct color types and are always "monolexemic"—that is, single words (Berlin and Kay 1969). If we were not English speakers, we would know that the basic level terms of the taxonomy refer to distinct colors, but we would have no way, from the taxonomic information, to determine the actual color.

At the terminal or "subordinate" level, we find less familiar and infrequently used terms that are often compound words. The compound tends to include the basic level term with a qualifier. The subordinate level term is a variant of the basic level term and adds only a bit more information. For instance, in the compound "bloodred," "red" provides most of the information we need to know about the color "bloodred." The subordinate level reflects the breadth or range of redness within the basic color category. The breadth of a basic or subordinate taxonomic level indicates the degree of interest members of a culture have concerning that domain (Kronenfeld 1996:49). For example, snowboarders and skiers know all sorts of terms for different kinds of snow, while those who have no interest in snow have only a few ("snow" and "*?$%#! Snow").

Most taxonomies are two to three levels deep; some have a depth of five or six levels, but this is unusual. The deeper a taxonomy—the more levels of inclusion—the greater the complexity of the concept. The taxomony for "kinds of social scientists" has six levels of inclusion, and if we follow just one of these taxonomic branches we would get (including the level [1] "social scientists"): (2) anthropologists, (3) sociocultural anthropologists, (4) psychological anthropologists, (5) cognitive anthropologists, and (6) cultural-model anthropologists. At each level we increase the degree of specialization and the complexity of the category "social scientist."

Paradigms/Componential Analysis

A taxonomy of pets tells us that cats and dogs are kinds of pets, but does not tell us *how* they differ. A paradigm, or componential analysis, does. The notion of paradigms came out of structural linguistics, particularly phonology—the study of the sounds of a language. For example, in describing how English speakers distinguish between a "p" and a "b," one needs to compare all the physical operations that go into producing these two sounds. Vocalizing both letters involves closing the lips, keeping the tongue flat and out of the way, and opening the lips with a little explosion of air. The difference is that one adds an "explosion of air" to the "p" sound and not to "b" sound. "Closed lips," "explosion of air," and "voice" are all *distinctive features* that one uses to descriptively compare these two sounds. The "meaning" of the sound "p" or "b" is an outcome of the conjunction of its component distinctive features. For example, "p" and "b" share two of these three distinctive features, more than either of them share with "a" or "r"; therefore we can infer that they are closer to each other in "sound meaning" than they are to either "a" or "r." Note that each of the three distinctive features has two alternative positions: (1) open versus closed mouth, (2) voiced versus voiceless and (3) explosion of air (aspiration) and no explosion of air. Each distinctive feature is structurally viewed as a semantic node along a *contrast set* (usually, but not necessarily, the end point). Thus, the voiced/voiceless pairing is called a contrast set while the "voiced" or "voiceless" options represent two alternative distinctive features within the contrast set.

The use of a distinctive features approach to analyze cultural categories (or concepts) is called a componential analysis. When (assumptively) all the distinctive features that comprise the meaning of a category are represented in diagram form, they constitute a "paradigm." A paradigm is a complete componential analysis of a category.

For example, suppose we consider the distinctive features of the category "Deadheads" (the devoted fans of the rock band The Grateful Dead). Long hair as opposed to short hair might be one distinctive feature, but hair color would not be a distinctive feature because it is not a *criterial attribute* that helps us decide whether X is or is not a Deadhead. Thus, a distinctive feature has to be an important (i.e., *salient*) component of the meaning of the term; if it isn't a salient component, then it is wrong to include it in our paradigmatic analysis of what Deadhead means.

Through interviews, we are likely to discover that Deadheads are considered "laid-back" and "noncompetitive" rather than "hyper" and "competitive." The set of distinctive features associated with Deadheads would represent one end of these two contrast sets, while the conjunction of the distinctive features on the other end of these contrast sets would represent another subcultural category (Republicans?). We can add more distinctive features, but this partial analysis shows that the function of a paradigm is to make explicit those salient underlying features that are associated and give meaning to a social category like Deadheads.

Table 3.2 is a partial componential analysis of the concept of "social affinity." Unlike taxonomies, the vertical dimension does not specify levels of inclusion. The componential analysis shows how the constellation of relational terms (mother, spouse, etc.) can be distinguished and cate-

Table 3.2.
Example of a Paradigm with Two Contrast Sets of "Social Affinity"

SOCIAL AFFINITY		
	BLOOD TIES	NON-BLOOD TIES
VERY CLOSE	Mother, father, brother, sister, son, daughter	Spouse/lover
CLOSE	Collateral kin: Uncles, aunts, first cousins	Friends, colleagues
NEUTRAL	Distant relatives you see occasionally	Acquaintances, superiors and subordinates
DISTANT	Relatives you never see	Strangers

gorized in terms of the respective conjunction of distinctive features from two contrast sets. One contrast set consists of a simple dichotomy—blood ties and no blood ties; the other consists of a continuous variable that ranges from "very close" to "distant." This paradigm offers a general sketch of what kinds of people we are close to and what kinds we are not. I emphasize that paradigms should be built from the bottom up, by eliciting relational terms (or whatever semantic domain you are interested in) through structured interviews (e.g., "what people are you close to?" and "how are you related to each?") rather than created ad hoc, as the above example was. Note that a side benefit of this form of analysis is that it is open to critical inspection by the readers; it is democratic.

Marking Hierarchies

These are a variant of taxonomies and the least studied of the cognitive structures.[3] I include them because they provide a unique and nonobvious insight into the meaning of many words. A simple marking hierarchy consists of two words with the "unmarked" word standing for both the category label and its most general and frequently used case. The "marked" word is the less general, less used case. David Kronenfeld (1996:97–98) uses the example of *cow* and *bull* where *cow* is both the category label that includes *cows* and *bulls* and that stands for the most general member of the category: the female *cow*. This relationship is diagrammed in figure 3.1.

Marking hierarchies are pervasive in human thinking because they economize the mental labor needed for thinking (i.e., the "cognitive workload") and for communicating. They do this by allowing one word to stand for two taxonomic levels of inclusion and also to stand for both members of one taxonomic level under "neutral conditions" (Greenberg 1966:25). We need only to specify that the cow is a bull when there is a reason to *mark* a cow as a bull. Similarly, consider the default settings of your word-processing program: the page size is set to "letter size" (8.5 x11 inches) unless otherwise specified and oriented to "portrait" rather than "landscape." These default settings save you time because you do not need to set page size or orientation unless the less typical setting is required.

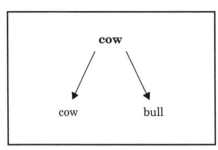

Figure 3.1. Marking Hierarchy for Cow

This same reliance on using a default (i.e., "unmarked") term to stand for less typical terms is evident in our use of measurement terms. For the following—length, *long / short*; height, *high / low*, *tall / short*; depth, *deep / shallow*; size, *big / small*, *fat / thin*—we use the unmarked terms (*high, tall, depth, big, far,* and *fat*) to ask questions about length, height, depth, distance, and size under neutral conditions. We ask how "deep is the pool?", not "how shallow?" Only under non-neutral conditions do we ask, "is that pool as shallow as the other one?" Why is this?

Kronenfeld (1996) speculates that the unmarked terms represents one cognitive assessment—some undefined distance from a zero point—while the marked term involves two cognitive assessments—one involving a move from a zero point *out* and the second involving a move back *toward* the zero point. Shallow, for example, involves two mental calculations. The first notes depth from a zero point and then, because it is shallow, an assessment of depth relative to the zero point. Hence, unmarked terms are more frequently used because they involve less mental sweat as they involve only a generic measure away from a zero point.

Think about the traditional use of "man" and "woman." Man has been the unmarked term referring to both "man" and "woman" as in "one giant step for mankind." Everyday language use of the man–woman marking hierarchy (and variants thereof) offers evidence of the infusion of patriarchal values in everyday speech. For example, at a recent dinner party I carelessly asked a man working in human services who had been talking about his supervisor, "Is he a good boss?" The man replied, "My boss is a woman, not a man." Whoops!

When I was a high school swim coach for the "girls' team," I used "guys" as a sexually neutral term to refer to "girls" or "women." In other words, I could say, "You guys are pathetic!" and sound a little less sharp, for "guys" is often used to address sexually mixed groups as well as all male ones. But look at the use of "guys" as part of a marking hierarchy: "Guys" contrasts with "gals," but "guys"—not "gals"—has become the default term that we use to refer to both males and females. Thus, "guys" is structurally equivalent to "men" and just as sexist. And how about the term "gays"? Gays refers both to "gays"—that is male homosexuals and lesbians, but lesbians specifies female homosexuals and does not in its regular usage extend to include male homosexuals. These sexist marking hierarchies are extensions of the man–woman marking hierarchy.[4]

Criticisms of These Early Approaches and the Demise of Ethnoscience

By the late 1960s, interest in ethnoscience began to wane as anthropologists and students criticized the profound (read, "pompous") claims and seemingly trivial results of cognitive anthropologists. "Who," to paraphrase what one colleague recently said, "gives a damn how the Tzetzal categorize firewood while their lives are short and brutish?" Of course, one might add that for a Tzetzal knowing good from bad firewood is very important to survival.

More reasoned criticisms from "within" led to serious internal hemorrhaging. Robert Randall (1976) observed that taxonomies depended on transitive logic to make indirect connections between the various hierarchical levels. For example, if a white oak is a kind of an oak and an oak is a kind of a tree, then it follows that a white oak is also a kind of a tree (this relationship is referred to as "indirect precedence" as opposed to the direct precedence of the "oak–tree" relationship). But, Randall observed, sometimes this is not the case. For example a *scrub oak* is a kind of an *oak,* but it is also a kind of a *bush.* This results in figure 3.2, which confounds the oak–tree path by adding another option.

How does this happen, and why doesn't this cause a "does-not-compute" message in our mind? Taxonomic structures often imply a cognitive confusion that in actuality does not occur. Taxonomies are built out of a sequence of vertical "either/or" relationship, where X (the terminal/subordinate level) is a kind of Y (the basic level) *only* and not a kind of Y and *also* a kind of Z (another basic level category).

There is also the problem of covert categories. Take cats and dogs: taxonomically, we can say that a lion is more like a cat than it is like a dog because they are included in the higher level "cat." In this instance, the taxonomic structure mirrors our psychological reality—that is, our general assessment that lions are more similar to cats than dogs. But how about wolves? We consider wolves to be much closer to dogs than to cats but, unlike the cat label for cats and lions, we don't have a common category label to represent a taxonomic node that includes both dogs

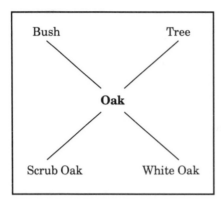

Figure 3.2. Taxonomy of Oaks
(Adapted from Randall 1976)

and wolves. Therefore, the taxonomic structure implies, wrongly, that dogs, cats and wolves are equally different from each other. This point was also made by Anthony Wallace and John Atkins (1969) who argued that taxonomic structures do not necessarily correspond to psychological reality. For instance, for an anthropologist, *"the English term cousin means any nonlinear consanguineal relative who is a descendent of a sibling of an ancestor of ego . . .'* but this is not what it means for any normal person" (p. 364; italics in original). They conclude that the taxonomic, structural descriptions of categories elicited by anthropologists are really the product of *behavior* produced by the informants in the *context* of the interview situation, which is, by definition, not typical of everyday situations.

Randall criticizes most ethnoscientists for considering taxonomies and other cognitive structures to be set in stone, changing, if at all, over generations and not in days or across contexts. Instead, he argues that taxonomies are constantly being updated and revised by new information and must be responsive to contextual cues. In the real world life is in flux, and taxonomies, if they are to be useful, must be flexible rather than rigid. Ethnoscientists had been using the Linnean taxonomy of living things as their template for what constitutes a taxonomy, an expert system, and not what most people use in their everyday life. Therefore, we should see how taxonomies of things like "oak" are adapted to suit particular *uses* like "sitting under" and "finding" them in the woods. The function of a cognitive structure is to store information efficiently for our use. The use of structures varies by context and interest. Consequently, Randall suggested that taxonomies tend to "dwarfism"—that is, small modular structures that we can mentally shuffle about as needed.

If you put your mind to it, there are quite a few things that can be put into taxonomies. But most things can't. Early ethnoscientific research focused on names (or pronouns), but what of all those nouns (not to mention nonverbal meanings) that are not names? What kind of taxonomic structure would we construct for "computer"? What would be its category and terminal labels? Or for "clouds"? No doubt there are ways we could create taxonomies, but the purpose of taxonomic structures is to make thinking easy, not difficult. Taxonomies are, however, particularly useful for biological categories.

The main problem was that ethnoscientists presumed that the

meaning revealed by taxonomic or paradigmatic structures of categories were equivalent to the way human beings used and understood them (that is, the psychological reality of the category) and that the structural properties mirrored the properties of meaning. But language is a symbol system, meanings of terms are ambiguous, contingent, negotiable, fluid. Wallace and Atkins (1969:355) pointed out the problem of "synonymy," where "father, dad, daddy, pop, and old man" are all identical in their literal or denotative criterial attributes (e.g., "male, one generation above ego, lineal") but certainly have different connotative meanings. We also have the inverse problem where "father" can refer to a religious status, God, or to an act (e.g., to "father" a bill through congress). Taxonomies and paradigms cannot help us analyze common metaphors such as "the sunset of life." For most purposes, humans use more flexible cognitive processes than those identified by these early ethnoscientists.

These criticisms of ethnoscience point out the limitations of the approach, but they do not undermine its usefulness when appropriate. Randall's proposal that we consider "dwarfish" modular taxonomies (and paradigms) that are malleable and sensitive to contexts offers a solution to the criticism that taxonomies and paradigms are decontextualized constructs and therefore cannot reflect the activities of our very contextualized psyches. It seems to me that marking hierarchies, taxonomies, and componential analysis remain powerful and useful ethnographic techniques that have been rejected by most anthropologists much too quickly and should remain in our methodological tool kit.

PROTOTYPES AND GRADED CATEGORIES

In 1969 Berlin and Kay laid the groundwork for a new way to conceive of the "psychological reality" of meaning. Using an array of 320 Munsell color chips, each representing a different color hue, they wanted to see whether color terms in different languages affected perceptions of color. They gave twenty foreign students, each a speaker of a different native language, two tasks. For the first task informants were asked to trace a boundary around "all those chips you would under any conditions call x" (a basic color term); in the second they were asked to point to the chip that is "the best, most typical example of x."

The first task was intended to get at the judged breadth or semantic extension of a basic color term, and the second task was intended to identify focal or core examples of each color. The results of the first task showed that there was great variation in determining the boundaries of a color term. Not only did speakers of different languages disagree with one another, but when asked to do the task again, they were likely to draw different boundaries than they did the first time.

In the second task, however, there was general agreement over the choice of the color chip that best corresponded to the informants' notion of that basic color term. Further studies demonstrated that there is wide cross-cultural agreement on the exemplary, or prototypical, member of each of the basic color terms. Everywhere, people tend to agree about what is the most typical or best example of red, blue, yellow (or other basic terms), but there is wide disagreement cross-culturally (and within cultures) about the extension of redness along a color spectrum. Their results indicate that the semantic space of a category has an internal structure that is built around a core *prototype*—the most codable (i.e., recognizable) member of the category. As one moves further from the prototype, terms become less codable. For example, as one moves from the prototype red to more yellowish reds, it becomes more difficult to decide whether the color should be coded as "red" or as "orange." Category boundaries are "fuzzy" and indeterminate rather than sharp and discrete. That is, there is no sharp boundary where people agree that "red" ends and "orange" begins.

Berlin and Kay's research stimulated new research on color terminology and the semantic structure of categories. Their study demonstrated that meaning was not always particulate—that is, located at the intersection of distinctive features—but often "graded" along a continuum in semantic space, with items in the space closer to the center being more easily identifiable as members of that category. Metaphorically the semantic space of a category is organized like the solar system; the focal referent or prototype serves as the "sun," and all other items that fall within the prototypes' gravitational (i.e., semantic) pull are thought to be more or less good members of that category. The color red is not just represented by one color but ranges from a dark purplish red to a light yellow red, with the quality of "redness" extending across the breadth of this semantic field.

A prototype model of meaning differs from a componential or taxonomic model of meaning, for the prototype is viewed as a gestalt or holistic image from which one makes assessments as to how well other items or things correspond with the prototype. The prototype is a mental image that, in a sense, is formed by mentally *averaging* all the most typical features important in identifying members of a particular category. James Boster (1988), for example, shows how the prototypical bird in northern California is defined in terms of the average features of birds of the *passerine* order, the largest order of birds in the area (it includes blue jays, robins, sparrows).

Eleanor Rosch (1975, 1978) developed the prototype theory of meaning through a series of innovative experiments. She asked students to rate, on a 7-point scale, the protoypicality, or best example, of instances of various categories. "Robin" was rated as the best example of bird and "penguin" the worst; "car" was rated the best example of a "vehicle." She hypothesized that there would be a direct correlation between an item's closeness to a prototype and how fast information about that item is "processed." Subjects were asked to identify pictures of various items, and their reactions were timed. Their (correct) responses were significantly faster for category members (such as robins) closer to the prototype than for those more distant. A second hypothesis she tested was that the better members of a basic level category should be more "substitutable" for the superordinate term of a category (e.g., "bird" is the superordinate term and robin and penguin the basic level terms) than the poorer members. For example, in the statement "twenty birds are perched on the wire" one can substitute "sparrows" for "birds," but it would be "ludicrous" to substitute "penguin"or "turkey" (Rosch 1975:191). Other experiments showed that the closer an item was to the prototype, the easier it was to learn and the more one could say about it or do with it (Rosch and Rosch 1978).

Rosch's conclusions are similar to those of Berlin and Kay for color but, importantly, they are generalized to all prototypes. She concluded that prototype-like members of a category have high "cue validity" to the "perceived world." That is, prototypes are composed of those cues (or clues) that most easily and quickly allow us to identify an item as a member of a category. For example, we know that feathers, wings, and beaks are good, valid perceptual cues for the category "birds." Rosch and Rosch write that "by prototypes of categories we have generally meant the clearest cases of membership defined operationally by people's judgments of goodness of membership in the category" (1978:36).

Prototype analysis need not be confined to object categories. Fehr and Russell (1991) are among the many researchers who have used prototype analysis to study emotions. In their study of love they had respondents "free list" all the types of love they could; they obtained a list of over 140 terms. They then asked students to rate, on a 1 to 6 scale, the prototypicality of 20 types of love. Among the most prototypical types of love were (in order of rating) *maternal love, parental love, friendship, sisterly love, romantic love*; among the lowest ratings were *sexual love, patriotic love, love of work, puppy love* and (last) *infatuation* (p. 428). They followed Rosch and her associates' methods and found that reaction times were quicker for those kinds of love rated high on protoypicality than for those rated low.

In another experiment meant to parallel Rosch's 1975 experiment on substitutability, students were asked to generate 10 sentences on love. From a list of 20 sentences such as "Love has to be worked at and strived for to be truly achieved," Fehr and Russell substituted the high prototypical kinds of love and the low prototypical kinds of love for the term "love" and asked students to rate on a 1 to 6 scale how "natural or peculiar" the sentence sounded to them. They hypothesized that the sentences with high prototype substitutions would sound more natural than those with low prototype substitutions. This hypothesis was borne out— for example, if you substitute "infatuation" for love in the above sample sentence, you can see that this is not a surprising outcome.

Fehr and Russell noted that ordinary folk and psychologists have very different conceptions of love and concluded that their research "suggest[s] that love is organized around several prototypes: love of a parent for a child, love between romantic partners, love between old friends . . . whereas psychologists have looked for one or two defining features of love, the folk definition of love is complex and provides no sharp boundary between love and other related experiences" (1991:435).

Summary of Prototype Research

A prototype communicates a bundle of qualities that together constitute the core meaning of a semantic domain (like "love" or "birds"). These qualities are thought of as dimensions that extend out like a gradient from the prototype. The extension of these dimensions from the prototype are said to structure and define a semantic space. Kronenfeld (1996) suggests that three basic or universal dimensions are significant for understanding semantic or meaning extensions from the core: shape, composition, and function. Shape and composition are important for referring to the *denotative*, literal, extensions from a prototype. The functional dimension is important for identifying the *connotative* extensions from a referent. Kronenfeld notes that the functional dimension is particularly important for understanding analogy and metaphor. For example, a straight-back wooden chair is probably many people's prototype for the category "chair." Neither a trash can, the floor, nor a table is shaped like a chair, and they are probably not composed of the same material, but they have the chairlike function of "sittability"; hence they are more chairlike than, say, a wooden spoon. These extensional dimensions of a prototype allow us to analyze metaphors in which the dimensional attributes of one semantic domain (or category) are mapped onto those of another domain. We now have the conceptual tools to analyze the metaphor "the sunset of life" by considering the functional dimension of "sunset" (the ending of the day) and mapping it on to "life."

Prototypes are produced out of our perceptions and experiences in the world. They demonstrate (except to postmodernists) that the real world has a correlational structure and is not just a chaotic jumble of events and things to which we give order through culture. Prototypes imply that order is imposed on our minds through our recognition of patterns that exist in our social and natural environments.[5] Prototypes provide *"maximum information with the least cognitive effort"* (D'Andrade 1995:115).

A prototype analysis is not an analysis of the flow of ideas and feelings one has, or of the flow of events and activities. Meaning is made fluid in prototype analysis but remains yoked to words. Schemas and cultural models extend the basic theoretical insights of prototype theory to mental narratives and the flow of behavior.

THE SCHEMA CONCEPT

In anthropology, schema theory rose out of the ashes of the earlier ethnoscientific approach. In psychology, Rosch and her associates had developed prototype theory that stemmed directly from the basic color category research of Berlin and Kay, both anthropologists. Prototype theory did not have the momentum to generate a flurry of research activity in anthropology. My guess is that this was simply because anthropologists, particularly cognitive anthropologists, were tired of being criticized for being fixated on words and categories at the expense of the flow of life in other cultures. The cool formality, the laboring over prototypes, did not appeal to the deeply romantic soul of most anthropologists.

Prototype theory provided a bridge to connect cognition with culture. But it was not until the growth of schemas, cultural models (a cultural model is a schema that is shared by a significant number of people in a society), and connectionist theory in the mid-1980s that this bridge received much traffic. This trinity—or monster, depending on your perspective—gave anthropologists the tools to explore the flow of meaning in everyday life. The consolidation and growth of schema theory in anthropology should largely be attributed to the efforts of Naomi Quinn and Roy D'Andrade.[6]

The term "schema" was first used by Sir Frederic Charles Bartlett (1932) and Jean Piaget (1970).[7] Bartlett defined schema as "an active organization of past reactions, or of past experiences, which must always be . . . operating in any well-adapted organic response" (1932:201). Piaget defined schema as "a cognitive structure which has reference to a class of similar action sequences, these sequences of necessity being strong, bonded totalities in which the constituent behavioral elements are tightly interrelated" (quoted in Flavell 1963:186).[8]

What these definitions have in common is that a schema is not just a picture in the head waiting to be mapped onto incoming perceptions, but it is a particular organization of memories that engage the present in a dynamic feedback loop. Unlike prototypes, schemas are not locked into words as their design elements; they can also be constructed out of images and logical operations. Though schemas still privilege language, their raison d'etre is to mediate and make sense (and sometimes nonsense) of the relationship between the individual (as a private and social self) and society. Schemas simultaneously "reconstruct" the past and present so that we are neither pawns of the past nor completely in thrall to the immediacy of the present.

In this brief exploration, I will describe seven different studies to give an idea of the flexibility and power of this approach. The seven studies represent very different, but compatible, uses of the schema concept.

Each represents a type of schema used to analyze a particular problem. The discussions on propositional schemas and analogical reasoning are more extensive and general because they are, it seems to me, glimpses of new and exciting theoretical vistas. The seven schema types we will discuss are: (1) *scripts,* as developed by Roger Schank and Robert Abelson; (2) the use of *metaphors,* as schemas for reasoning by Naomi Quinn; (3) an analysis of the *narrative structure* of a Mexican folktale to describe gender schemas by Holly Mathews; (4) examples of the use of *propositional schemas* in everyday life to communicate cause-and-effect relations by Roy D'Andrade and Ed Hutchins; (5) the use of *narratives analysis* and schema theory by Linda Garro; (6) *personal semantic network* connectionist-schemas to discuss how motivations and values are tied together by Claudia Strauss; and (7) *analogical thinking* as described by Bradd Shore and Douglas Hofstadter.

Scripts

In the 1970s Schank and Abelson sought to take a computational "Artificial Intelligence" approach out of the lab and into the streets. They wanted to develop a theory that "provides a meaning representation for events. Here we are concerned with the intentional and contextual connections between events, especially as they occur in human purposive action sequences" (1977:4). They wanted to discover and make formally explicit the "theoretical entities" that organize "episodic memory" that they defined as memory "organized around personal experiences or episodes rather than around abstract semantic categories" (p. 17).

Memory is not made by some behind-the-eyes-and-ears director zealously transcribing and storing experiences on memory reels. Instead meaning and memory, like the two hands of a seamstress, knit experiences into schemas. Behind the schemas (to extend the metaphor) are the goals and intentions, the desires and skills of the seamstress. Similarly, each individual knits his or her own schemas out of his or her daily experiences.

Scripts are formulaic schemas. A script consists of all the knowledge you need to act appropriately in a given situation (p. 37). Scripts refer to very specific and usually culturally shared sequences of events that form "bonded totalities." Simple examples of scripts are going to a restaurant, getting gas, going to the supermarket, and for some, getting drunk at a party. Each of these events consists of a fairly formulaic and specific set of activities that have a beginning (entering), and an ending (leaving, heaving). Because scripts are "intersubjectively shared" —we know that other people are familiar with these scripts—we usually just signal a script sequence in conversations and get on to the more interesting "stuff." We do not, for example, bother describing our dining experience at Wendy's. Schank and Abelson state that "most of our understanding" of the world is script based (p. 67). Script analysis is about "filling in" what's left out of the script signal. What do you have to fill in, in order to make sense of the statement "I went to Wendy's for the salad bar"? What would be the expected, typical order of behaviors in this script, and what would not fit? It would make no sense for someone to "fill in," I drank champagne and bought a mattress at Wendy's." It would make sense to infer that: "I was hungry and wanted a quick, cheap meal that was relatively healthy; I paid for the food with money; I served myself and ate off a plate with a plastic fork," and so on. Normally, one doesn't fill in the details because the script is a precoded "bonded totality."

How about this script, taken from Schank and Abelson: "John went to a park. He asked the midget for a mouse. He picked up the box and left" (1977:40). We are confused both by the definite article "the" preceding "midget" and "box" and by the last two sentences. The two "thes" imply that John was on a mysterious mission and went specifically to meet a midget for a mouse (perhaps to feed the cobra in his closet?). And somebody left him a "box" (perhaps to keep the cobra in?). "Sitting on a bench and reading" or something like that should follow the script line "went to a park." Schemas as mental configurations anticipate certain sequences of actions and can stay in the "sleep mode" as long as those expectations are met, but must become alert and dynamic when surprises occur. Analogous to Katherine P. Ewing's 1990 explanation of the self, only inconsistencies, deviations from the script, jar us into realizing that behaviors—ours and others'—are mostly scripted.

Schema Hierarchies and Motivations

What motivates a person to adopt one schema as opposed to another? At one level, schemas interpret contextual and behavioral cues in order to cue up the appropriate behavioral response. But that leads to viewing schemas as stimulus-response mechanisms that people use to identify social stimuli and respond appropriately. Instead, schemas also incorporate motives for directing behavior toward higher-level goals that transcend situations. Roy D'Andrade (1992; 1995) writes that schemas are hierarchically organized (not unlike taxonomies and prototypes). He refers to top-level schemas as "master motives" defined as personal goals that the individual holding them believes are intrinsically worthwhile pursuing: love, knowledge, or art for example. In turn, master motives "instigate" lower, basic-level schema, which, in turn, instigate yet lower subordinate-level schemas. Master level motives, like "success," may be universal (D'Andrade did not speculate) but, even so, the particular goals and understandings of success are shaped through personal experiences as a member of a particular society. Here the social and the individual interpenetrate; after all, a member of a foraging society can neither want to be nor become a proctologist. For Westerners, success may mean making big bucks, getting married and raising a family, surfing, or becoming a survivalist in Idaho.

The "master-level schema" of success does not stipulate what success is; instead, it describes how success organizes lower-level, goal-striving activities. Success doesn't just happen. One has to do something, like go to class and study hard. Studying hard (for most) is not a motivation in itself. One studies hard in order to get good grades in order to become (say) a doctor. The "wanting to be a doctor" is a basic-level schema that explains why the person studied hard and received high grades. But why would someone want to become a doctor? Two reasons come to mind: one, the person wants a job that ensures financial security and wealth; second, one finds deep satisfaction in curing the sick. Thus, healing and wealth are potential master-level motivational schemas.

Naomi Quinn (1992) has used and added on to D'Andrade's approach to schemas. Two of her many contributions to the above model are: (1) her focus on the ways in which schemas become shared and thus, serve as cultural models and (2) her demonstration of the ways that metaphors communicate the underlying motivational force, content and conditionals of schemas.

A straightforward reason that schemas are shared is that "the world is organized in exactly such a way as to ensure that people will have the same experiences" (Quinn 1992:187–188). Metaphors in particular serve as a "shared fund of cultural exemplars" that, like scripts, "stand for various agreed-upon features of the world." For example, Quinn found that two of the most popular types of metaphors for American marriage are that it is "a manufactured product" and that it is "a journey." The "manufactured product" metaphor fits both the cultural ideal that a good marriage lasts a lifetime and the Protestant ethic that a couple should work hard to make their marriage successful. In this metaphorical schema, marriage is objectified as a product that, if a couple puts in the effort, commitment, and work, will be a quality product that lasts. The master motive of success is incorporated into the schema for marriage through various "manufactured product" types of metaphors.

Dorothy Holland (1982:80–81) argues that motivations and schemas must always be tied into a self-schema that "identifies" and "internalizes" other schemas. She adopted Spiro's (1982:48) description of five levels of cognitive salience to the different levels that a schema may be internalized. The idea is that the deeper a schema is internalized, the greater one self-identifies with it, and the greater the motivational force of the schema. Take the example of marriage: at the first level of internalization, a person learns about the schema for marriage; at the second, a person comes to understand what the schema is about; at the third, the person believes that this is a part of life that s/he will pass through; at the fourth level, the schema for marriage begins to influence and guide the person's actions—the person *wants* to get married; and at the fifth and deepest level of internalization, the person's actions are directly motivated by his or her desire to get married—marriage is not only the "right thing to do," but the "natural" thing to do.

Quinn shows that married individuals, particularly wives, often act in ways that are not dictated by any obvious cost-benefit analysis of self-interest because they have internalized the desire to make their marriage a success. Her informants' references to "sticking it out" and "working together" point to how culturally shared images and values are packaged into metaphors that are used to guide action and to think about relationships and marriage.

On the other hand, other values and images are incorporated into metaphors that undermine the above metaphors. For example, "therapeutic" metaphors related to self-fulfillment (e.g., "we've become so stagnant") and romantic love (e.g., "the spark has gone out of our marriage") can be used to justify divorce (Ilouz 1997). Love is usually the master-level motive and marriage the basic-level motive—Heather married Jason *because* she loved Jason (as opposed to an arranged marriage where Heather loves Jason because she married him). If Heather ceases to love Jason, then the most salient reason for the marriage is gone, and conflict, unhappiness and perhaps divorce ensue. Quinn's research shows how we use metaphors to live and reason by.

Teaching Cultural Models Through Folktales

Instead of discovering schemas through metaphors or scripts, Mathews (1992) focused on one Mexican folktale: *La Llorona*, "The Weeping Woman." Mathews collected 60 accounts of this folktale in a Mexican community and found that when her male and female informants recounted the story, they told it differently and extracted different morals from it. Here are two of the versions Mathews collected. (See if you can figure out which is told by a male and which by a female.)

> **Story 1**. La Llorona was a good girl who married an older, more experienced man. They had children, and she worked hard. But one day she found out that he was seeing another woman and that he was giving money to this woman to build a house. She had much shame (*pena*) and did not know what she should do. So she followed him to the woman's house, confronted them both and cursed him for neglecting his family. And he said to her, "Are you satisfied to shame me in front of the town? What kind of a man do you think I am that I would let you curse me in this way? I do not want you to enter my house again. You are no longer the mother of my children. Go, leave my house, and see if you can find anyone to take you in." And so she went to the river and drowned herself. And now she helps us, too, on dark nights by leading men who are not home with their families to drown in the river.

Story 2. Well, it begins like this. There was a woman who married a man. The man married her because she was a decent girl from a good family. They had four children, but then she did not want more. So she became cold (*se puso frio*) to him (i.e., stopped having sex with him). The husband had to look elsewhere for his needs. He found another woman. His wife became enraged (filled with *coraje*). She confronted him, but he would not listen to her. So she killed herself and her children so that he would not have a home and family. But now this evil woman can never go to Heaven. She must spend her days and nights wandering forever.

These tales describe the morality requirements of husbands and wives and the consequences of immoral behavior. In both tales, it is the wife who drowns herself. In the first story, revenge is gained posthumously as faithless and negligent husbands are led by la Llorona to drown in a river. In the second tale, the husband's infidelity is presented as a reasonable response to his wife's "coldness." Her refusal to have sex with him leads to her being portrayed as evil with its inevitable consequences: death and eternal damnation. The moral is obvious.

Mathews investigated the grammatical structure of these tales in order to make explicit the rules her informants used to bead the actions together into a believable and coherent story. Meaning is not just communicated through the words themselves, but also through the formal rules (i.e., the grammar) that govern the order of plot moves in a story. From her analysis, Mathews identified the following generic and generative narrative structure: each story has a *setting* and an *episode*. The setting consists of an *introduction* of the main characters, the "locale," and, optionally, the "time." The episode consists of a *beginning*, a *development*, and an *end*. The beginning consists of a *precipitating event* and an *initiating event*. The precipitating event sets in motion the condition for the disruption of a cultural schema while the initiating event is the actual disruption "that elicits a response reaction from the protagonist . . . (i.e., the one who is wronged)" (1992:131). The development involves a *complex reaction* and a *plan*. The complex reaction consists of an *emotional response* by the protagonist to the initiating event and a *desire*. The plan involves a set of *reactions* or *actions* intended to satisfy the desire and the *consequences* of that action. The consequences may be the end of the story or may lead to a final *ending* and *outcome* that provide the moral of the story and a final-ending *event*. It is easier to see this structural schema in diagram form (see figure 3.3).

Each la Llorona story unfolds according to the pattern presented in figure 3.3. This structural schema does not depend on whether the story is told by a man or a woman. The structure gives "credibility" or "convincingness" to the story.

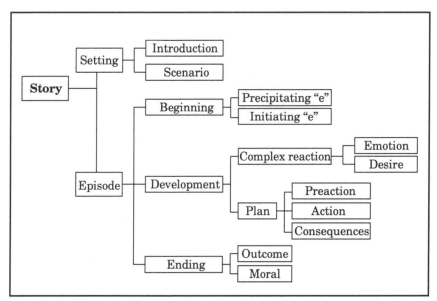

Figure 3.3. Mathews's Diagram for the Grammatical Analysis of La Llorona Folktales

Mathews's work is more obviously descended from the taxonomies and componential analysis of the old school than are the works of Quinn (1992) and D'Andrade (1992). The grammar of a folktale, Mathews notes (1992:129), is also a schema, linking events in a conditional loop of moves that progress to an ending (i.e., if a, then b; and if b, then c and so on, until the end). But we don't *notice* how the grammar works with the narrative content to create meaning (that is, the story). It is the very transparency of the grammar, providing a scaffolding for content, that makes people respond with who-needs-this? feelings or remarks. No doubt, Mathews has frequently received this kind of comment because she writes, "Some may wonder at the value of this exercise in formalism. Does it really shed light on cultural models of gender in the community as revealed in folktale, or are we simply performing complicated analyses that confirm what could be more directly learned through participant observation?" (p. 30).

But what if there were no grammar? For example, try to make sense of the following: "and clouds I while rained slept gathered it?" Not so easy. The point being that the "obvious" meaning of the story is not simply obtained through the word content but also through the grammar. The strength of Matthews's analysis is that it provides a single grammar that can be effectively applied to all sixty and potentially more versions of this folktale.

Propositional Schemas

We use schemas for purposes of reasoning. When we acquire new information, we apply a host of "living tools" to make sense of that information. In chapter 1, I argued that if you know someone's favorite actor is Sylvester Stallone and he is a hockey fan, then you are pretty sure he also likes steak and is unlikely to vote for an increase in the welfare budget. We infer that there is a relationship between statement ("my favorite actor is") and action (the person has seen movies by that actor, and people who like those movies also like to do x, y, and z).

Ed Hutchins (1980) points out that this mode of inferential reasoning—connecting belief and value statement to action—is itself a cultural schema. In logic, this kind of reasoning is called *modus pollens* and is presented as: "if p, then q; p." "P" and "q" are place holders, and we know that if we observe p, then q must also be present. For example, if p = "if it rains" and q = "the ground gets wet," we need not mention that "the ground gets wet when it rains." The logical operator—modus pollens—is verbalized only when we need to make that observation. It would seem that inferential reasoning is as innate a capacity as language. Even the squirrels around my bird feeder know that when I raise my hand, then there must be a rock that I am throwing at them, and they scurry away (some, realizing my bad aim, just continue pilfering the seed).

The contrapositive logical operator, called the *modus tollens* is presented as: "if p, then q; not q." To go back to the rain example, this rule states: "if it rains (p), then the ground gets wet (q); the ground is not wet (*not q*)." Has it rained? This is a slightly more difficult schema to learn. The reason is not unlike Kronenfeld's explanation for why we use "deep" rather than shallow as the default term for depth. For modus tollens, we first apply the modus pollens rule ("if p then q; p") and then have to go back to turn p into "not q." Thus, modus pollens is the default "basic level" propositional schema, while the modus tollens is a marked variant that increases the "toll" on our cognitive workload.

Because anthropologists are concerned with natural rather than purely formal learning, there has been some interest in investigating the use of propositional schemas cross-culturally. Hutchins (1980) sees propositions as the building blocks of culture. In *natural* reasoning, as opposed to formal reasoning, we use our knowledge and cultural beliefs and values to construct propositional schemas. For example, we may see that the sky is cloudy and therefore bring an umbrella with us when we go outside. The sequence of actions from first perceiving clouds to carrying an umbrella constitutes a propositional schema based on pragmatic inferential reasoning (Hutchins 1980; see also D'Andrade 1995).

Hutchins uses propositional schemas based on natural reasoning to show how Trobriand Islanders apply logical operators to present their case in local arguments over land rights. An example of a general schema looks like this: "[ ] ——U(g)———> [ ]"; where [ ] stands for individuals and U(g) for "someone allocates use rights in a garden to someone else" (1980:55). Propositions are generated from this schematic template by filling in the kinds of culturally relevant conditions under which some person can and cannot justifiably transfer land rights. For example, land is owned by the matriline, and ownership of land cannot be transferred, but use rights to garden lands can. In order to receive land, a man must give *pokala* to the matrilineal "owner" of the land. Pokala consists of a gift of various goods (bananas, fish, yams) to the matrilineal owner of the land. Two modus pollens propositional schemas are generated from these cultural axioms: (1) if one gives pokala and it is accepted, then one receives use rights to land; (2) if one "owns" land then one can transfer use rights to the land. Conflicts are expressed in forms such as denial of the antecedent (e.g., a claim that pokala was not given) and modus tollens (i.e., a claim that X did not possess use rights to land).

One important result of Hutchins's work was that it demonstrated that the Trobrianders use these logical operators just as we do as part of their day-to-day lives. Earlier, Dorothy Lee (1949) in an influential and fascinating article had suggested that the Trobrianders did not rely on causal reasoning. Instead they relied on a kind of image/imitative reasoning in which present-day actions and ideas mimic ancestral ideas and actions. In Arnold Modell's (1993) words, the Trobrianders, unlike "us," had not escaped the tyranny of time: past, present, and future reflect each other. Most critics of Lee's approach, however, conveniently forget that she did say that the Trobrianders do use causal reasoning; they just don't value it as much as we do.

Hutchins's work is profoundly important for two more reasons: (1) it shows that members of non-Western cultures use the same kind of logical operations that Westerners do; and (2) his detailed ethnographic study of a few Trobriand land disputes provides empirical support for the more general theoretical claim that propositional schemas are not only universal, but pervade everyday life in every culture.

Narrative Models of Meaning

Many of the schema and cultural model approaches can be construed as narrative forms of analysis. However, where schema and cultural model approaches seek to formulate abstract representations from "experience near" or survey data, narrative models do not "ascend to the abstract" but stay grounded in the concrete (Bruner 1986, cited in Mattingly and Garro 1994:771). In addition, while cultural models (and often schemas) lack a point of view, narratives are always told from a personal perspective and usually for the purpose of convincing the audience of the merit of the narrator's point of view. Elinor Ochs and Lisa Capps (1996) note that the world does not come precoded—we create or recreate the world and ourselves in our narratives. One way we do this is by "choosing" a perspective.

Another important feature of narratives is that they rely on "auto-biographical memory," which Garro writes is "best understood as reconstructions rather than reproductions of past events" so that "the present is explained with reference to the reconstructed past; and both are used to generate expectations about the future" (1994:776). Narratives, Garro reminds us, are mediated by schemas or cultural models. For Garro, narrative analysis is not (as I suspect it is for many) an easy way out of doing formal analysis but must incorporate both an analysis of schemas and an understanding of how memory works.

Illness narratives serve as a "vehicle" by which patients compare their experiences with the relevant cultural models and try to make sense of the contradictions that often arise between their experiences and their expectations (Garro 1994:778). What is striking about personal narratives is their "eventness," as informants recount the often dreadful and isolating experiences that they underwent and continue to undergo. As Mattingly and Garro put it:

> Narrative is used when we want to understand concrete events that require relating an inner world of desire and motive to an outer world of observable actions and states of affairs.
>
> Narrative offers what is perhaps our most fundamental way to understand life in time. Through narrative we try to make sense of how things have come to pass and how our actions and the actions of others have helped shape our history; we try to understand who we are becoming by reference to where we have been. (1994:771)

In her work on individuals afflicted with temporomandibular joint disorder (also known as TMJ, a condition characterized by chronic pain and/or stiffness in the temporomandibular joint in the lower jaw), Garro combines narratives with cultural models to show (1) how her informants used cultural models to make sense of their illness experiences, (2) how personal experiences clash and interact with cultural models, and (3) how changes in informants' illness experiences often led to selecting different cultural models or modifying old ones. What is important here is that Garro not only states that individuals consciously interact with cultural models to forge an understanding of their experiences but describes the often intense interaction between individual experiences and the cultural models they use to make sense of those experiences.

For example, a primary cultural model that her informants had to come to grips with was the mind–body dualism. Garro writes that "the dominant metaphor of biomedicine is the body as a biochemical machine" (1994:12); thus, the source of an illness is located either in the body or in the mind. If it is in the body, the patient copes by utilizing psychological distancing, sometimes to the point of denying that the body is part of the self. On the other hand, if the illness is thought to be in the mind, then the patient becomes responsible for his or her disease. For instance, doctors often doubted that the source of their patients' pain was exclusively somatic and therefore treated them (i.e., the informants) as if they were "crazy."

In most of the narratives, the patients came to accept a physically based TMJ model of their illness. They then began to focus on finding the most effective treatment strategies. As Garro notes, most informants typically described their body metaphorically, as "an object in need of fixing." For example, one informant said, "I am quite frustrated because my body doesn't want to cooperate with me." Another expressed how her illness limited her: "Pain dictates what I do and what I don't do." These narrative statements incorporate the mind–body cultural model by viewing the self as separate from and in conflict with the body.

Garro's narrative analysis is an advance over typical ethnographic analysis of informant narratives, which tend to be ad hoc. Indeed, her work contributes to the cultural model approach described above because anthropology, as opposed to psychology, is ultimately grounded in description and analysis of human life as it unfolds (and unravels) in everyday life. Narratives are not "life," but they are the prototypical means we use to make sense of our experiences.

Garro's analysis of narratives presents a theory of cultural models that differs from the one presented by Quinn (1992) and D'Andrade (1992) (though they are not incompatible). Most cultural model theorists, including Quinn and D'Andrade, use Spiro's (1987) five levels of cognitive salience to account for the motivational force of a cultural model. However, this approach implies that once a model has reached "level five" and is seen as "naturally instigating" behavior, there is no mechanism to reverse or diminish the motivational force of the internalized schema. At the deepest levels of internalization, the cultural model is, itself, reified as the agent of action, and the individual disappears (or becomes irrelevant) as the agent of action or inaction.

Garro's (1994) theory of cultural models does not rely on stages of internalization for explaining motivation. As I read her, narratives keep the informant central to the analysis, and therefore the cultural models remain *external* to the informant's predilections and motives. An informant-centered analysis of meaning entails that humans make meaning by using, molding, and sometimes discarding cultural models. The cultural models are never, in themselves, meaningful, until they are incorporated into narratives and acquire a point of view.

Personal Semantic Networks (Connectionist Theory)

Claudia Strauss (1992b; 1997) is to my knowledge the first anthropologist to combine connectionist (or neural network) theory with schema theory to analyze her ethnographic materials. Strauss worked with blue-collar workers at the Ciba-Geigy Ltd. chemical plant in Cranston, Rhode Island. Her article "What Makes Tony Run?" (1992b) will be the focus of this discussion; this study is based on interviews with five working-class men.

Strauss wanted to find out what these men's ideas of "success" were and assumed that the "master motive" for success would precipitate basic and lower-level motivations. She found that the men "easily verbalized values that underpin the 'American Dream': with hard work anyone in America can get ahead, and everyone should strive to do so" (1992b:199). Contrary to her expectations, this master motive did not have a strong motivational force. She referred to it as a "bounded" master motive that her informants paid lip service to, but one that had no relevance to their lives. On the other hand, the workers were motivated by "breadwinner values"—an unbounded schema that is connected to many other salient schemas (1992b:199). An "unbounded" schema is highly motivating because it is strongly identified with the self-schema and through that identification with a wide variety of different experiences and schemas. One usually does not self-identify with a bounded schema, even though it may be a master motive. As a result, bounded schemas are not connected, via the self-schema, to a wide range of experiences and, therefore, are seldom activated. To illustrate: you can wish to be an astronaut and do various things such as join an astronomy club, buy property on Mars from a real estate agent, but not let this motive infiltrate much else of your life. On the other hand, you can have a schema to "enjoy life" and have it influence most everything you do as you drop out of school.

The distinction between a bounded and an unbounded schema has not been brought up before. What happens when one has more than one master-level schema concerning the same arena of experience? The American dream motive suggests that one should continue working and striving to better oneself. The breadwinner role presents a *satisficing* rather than a *maximizing* motivational model of success, as one's occupational motives should revolve around feeding and caring for the well-being of one's family; everything else is gravy, "superfluous" surplus (Brown 1959).

To discover why the "breadwinner" schema as opposed to the "American Dream" schema had motivational saliency, Strauss (1992b) investigated the personal network of associations (or connections) each of these schemas had for the informant. In so doing, Strauss developed a more encompassing type of cognitive structure than can be built using schema theory alone by connecting schemas to one another. This move of combining schemas in a connectionist model is analogous to the move from taxonomies to prototypes and from prototypes to schemas.

Rather than looking for the core features of a term, connectionist theory looks at the *linkages* between units. Linkages have different strengths of associations activated either by a small impulse, such as "I'm hungry, let's eat," or a strong excitatory impulse, as in "I gotta study, the test is in two hours!" As Strauss writes, "in connectionist models *semantic information* (e.g., what love is) is not stored in anything like a dictionary, separate from *episodic information* (e.g., specific experiences of loving and being loved or not loved, reading and hearing about love, etc.)" (1992a:12). We may share similar ideas about what love means if we are asked to talk about "what love is," but attach different values to these features of love because of *how* we've experienced love. For example, we might all consider kissing or gift giving as prototypical expressions of love but disagree on their value to us because we might have had a lover who gave gifts all the while secretly pursuing someone else! Such episodic information influences our identification with what are otherwise prototypical features of a particular schema.

No two people have the same repository of experiences. As a result, even though they may share the same schemas for love and marriage, the pattern of connections are necessarily different and, consequently, so is the motivational force and meaning of these schemas for each person. The profound consequences of these ideas on social science research is that the research cannot presuppose the motivational force of a schema (or concept or attitude) on the basis of survey or other methodologies that only examine what an individual knows about a particular schema (concept or attitude). In order to evaluate the motivational saliency of any schema, the researcher has to discover the pattern of connections. Strauss refers to this pattern as the Personal Semantic Network (PSN): "idiosyncratic webs of meaning carried by each person, linking individually salient verbal symbols to memories of significant life experiences and conscious self-understandings" (1992b:211).

Her method for finding these links is based on three "aspects of discourse" that she finds "indicative of strong associations of cognition" (1992b:211). These are: (1) *Contiguity*—when idea A typically follows idea B in an interview, then they are semantically associated (e.g., "I was hungry, so I checked out the refrigerator for something, anything, to eat"); (2) *Significant terms*—when a term is used to describe both A and B, then A and B are associated with each other. For example if one uses the term "awesome" to describe both Tony's pizza and Tom Cruise (assuming that "awesome" is a significant term!); (3) *Shared "voice"*— two terms are semantically associated with each other when a person uses the same register of speech and voice to talk about both of them. For example, if one talks about the state of the world and one's marriage in the same dismal voice and outlook, then these two schemas are linked. I think this methodology is too vague to be widely implemented but that the idea of describing and analyzing personal semantic networks through connections between schemas and determining the relative strengths of those connections is correct.

Analogy Formation, the Construction of Meaning, and Creativity

Our final model for exploring the making of meaning comes from Bradd Shore's (1996) book *Culture in Mind*. Except for connectionist models of meaning, other approaches to the study of meaning have relied on analytic procedures to get at (1) the structural design, (2) the logical operators, and (3) the underlying features of one or more symbols. Shore argues that not all meanings are, as it were, analytically extracted from their communicative packet. Instead, he proposes that some meanings are born whole and simply cannot be taken apart. These meaning systems are actualized in their totality and do not originate in language.

Analogies such as "clouds are like sponges because clouds are soft and fluffy, and so are sponges," create a linkage between two distinct domains through a perceived *sensory* resemblance. Analogies, unlike analytical thinking, are built from "participatory" fields of meaning. The sponge–cloud analogy forms its own rich complex of meaning, created out of a synthesis where none had existed before; it cannot be understood through an analysis of its component parts. The simplest and most easily learned types of analogies are a product of "mimicry" or "simple imitation." But humans do not just imitate. Mimicry is intentional and, therefore, more than mere imitation. Shore introduces the relationship between memory and mimicry by recalling Plato's discourse on Meno's paradox. Meno (a Greek) asked Socrates, "But how will you look for something . . . when you don't in the least know what it is? How on earth are you going to set up something you don't know as the object of your search? To put it another way, even if you come right up against it, how will you know that what you have found is the thing that you didn't know?" (cited in Shore 1991:327). Socrates answered that all learning stems from remembering what you already know, that is, through creative and active mimicry. Analogy formations are making new, creative connections between things that you already know.

Thus far, Shore has set up two conditions for analogical reasoning: it connects present with past experiences, and the connection is based on a process of finding one or more similarities across independent semantic domains (clouds and sponges). The similarities, Shore claims, are often (though not always) arrived at through "nonanalytic" scanning. What does that mean?

At the lowest level of neural networks, connectionist models show that concepts are encoded as distributed networks of neural activations and inhibitions. The pattern is the meaning. In addition, the full pattern doesn't have to be realized—it only has to be partially or coarsely coded for it to be activated. Analogy formation depends, at this most elementary level, on sufficient pattern formation. For example, my act of "typing on the keyboard" involves a basic bodily mimicry of neural pattern formations that I am utterly unconscious of.

The neural level of connectionist theory is too low a level to explain a baseball game or laughter. Shore's purpose is to show how analogy formation moves up levels, from the biological to that of cultural models; to do so he makes a distinction between *"primary analogy formation"* and *"second-order analogies"* (1991:352). This is, I think, his most critical step, for nonanalytical meaning stems directly from primary analogy formation while feature/dimension types of analyses stem from second-order analogies. Shore notes that nonanalytic meaning consists of "'integral attributes' perceived as 'unitary wholes' rather than concatenations of separate attributes" (1991:355; Rosch and Rosch 1978 cited in Shore). As the meaning of a neural network *is* its pattern of associations, so nonanalytic meaning is realized in the whole (primary) analogy.

This is all a bit bizarre, but it becomes clearer when he discusses synesthesia. *Synesthesia* refers to "cross-modal perceptual identification" (Shore 1991:9); this means that one sense mode (say, sight) and another (auditory) are mutually activated by a particular sensory input. A high-pitched, sound, for instance, is identified with a light color and a low-pitched sound with a dark color. The mixing of temperature and color, as in "hot" and "cool" colors, is another example of synesthesia. Dwight Bolinger (1989, cited in Shore) has identified sets of words that share a common sound and evoke a common meaning that is not analytically grounded in the definitional attributes of the words themselves. An example of what he calls "phonosthemes" are *"-udge"* words such as *"fudge"*, *"trudge,"* *"budge,"* *"sludge,"* *"grudge"*—all of which convey a "heavy stickiness" (1996:359).

The importance of synesthesia to primary analogy formation is that it seems to be biologically rooted, nonanalytical (i.e., the meaning is just "there" and it is shared), and a type of analogy. The following multiple choice example helps make this point: red:blue: as —:—. (a) green:yellow, (b) high:low; (c) good:bad; (d) hot:cool. Shore (following Bolinger) claims that there is no logical reason for this shared association though it has a neurological basis as certain visual stimuli trigger similar responses in different cortical neurons (1996:358). Shore writes that "these nonanalytical processes are good candidates for elementary forms of meaning construction" (p. 359). The important point here is that analogy formation has a biological/neurological base and is rooted in personal embodied experiences. This foregrounds the importance of the body as well as the mind in the construction of meaning. But how do we get "culture in mind"?

From the above examples and argument, Shore concludes that humans have an innate capacity for *analogical schematization*: the process by which cultural models are translated into personal, mental models. Schematization is a process by which "concrete source models" (e.g., watching a basketball game) are simplified by filtering out what is, to the individual, insignificant in building a schematic analogue (1996:344). In analogical schematization, differences are eliminated and one scans for pattern similarities across schemas. Often the pattern relations are nonanalytic or poetic and figural. An interesting example Shore gives is that of a person channel surfing on the TV and the analogous image that it evokes of an alienated, solitary individual. The connection, according to Shore, is not accessible by conventional analysis until after both patterns are wholly mapped onto each other.

The most typical type of schematization occurs when we participate in an event and take it as indicative of that class of events—for instance, going to the opera, assuming that all opera performances are kindred spirits of this one, and, hence, that one need never go again. The analogy would look something like this, *opera:no fun::OPERA:NO FUN* (where the class–instance relationship, the activity opera, and its specific emotional response is in the lower case and the class-type in upper case). In this way cultural models can enter the mind through single-case experiences.

One of the more interesting cultural insights Shore derives from his theory of analogical schematization is the analogy between baseball and courtship ritual. Here the analogy involves mapping "foundational schemas" on to "institutional" cultural models. The foundational schema for baseball indicates how the game is organized around asymmetries in time and space: time is relative, as it is kept in innings rather than by a clock; and space is divided into odd numbers: three fields, three bases, nine innings, three outs, a seventh-inning stretch; and ballparks vary in size and shape. These (and other) fundamental asymmetries contrast with the symmetries of time and space in the world of basketball and football. Analogously, dating—located between childhood and marriage—is also made up of odd places and times, feelings and relations. Shore asserts that this mapping of asymmetries, of which we are normally unaware, explains why baseball expressions are often used to discuss the sexual tensions of dating. For example, we can say "I struck out" in reference to a date, but it sounds odd in reference to a spouse or friend. Through analogy schematization we see that both cultural models (baseball and courtship/dating) share a common foundational schema based on the symmetry/asymmetry contrast.

Analogy schematization can explain how cultural models change over time, that is, how meanings are born, are modified, and die. A new experience can be "accommodated" to fit an older model and in the process change it. For example, our novel experiences with the Internet have altered many of our models of shopping and socializing.

Shore argues that analogical schematization "mediates" the relationship between culture and mind. The feedback loop between culture and mind leads to a distributive network of meanings. Relations of meanings between words and things, sights and sounds, feelings and activities, and so on are conventionalized through their repeated associative use in social practices. However, these conventionalized associations are never imitatively "reborn" in the mind but are continually susceptible to modification by the very fact that analogical connections are always contingent and potentially creative. The conventional analogical schema is tweaked by the individual who sees connections from her own unique and zany perspective. What is important is not that patterns are "out there" waiting to be "found" and incorporated into the mind, but that we create the patterns by making connections between things that are not "logically" related (like clouds, numbers, and happiness—being on "cloud nine"); thus the patterns that we find in the world are the work of both the individual mind and culture.

Whereas Shore's approach to analogy formation is holistic, Douglas Hofstadter and his associates have been working on reproducing analogy formation through a computer program called "Copycat." Hofstadter criticizes connectionist models as pitched at too low a level of specificity:

> Trying to use connectionist language to describe creative thought strikes me as a bit like trying to describe the skill of a great tennis player in terms of molecular biology, which would be absurd. Even a description in terms of the activities of muscle cells would lie at far too microscopic a level. What makes the difference between bad, good, and superb tennis players requires description at a high functional level—a level that does not belong to microbiology at all. (1995:308)

Like Shore, Hofstadter argues that analogies are the foundation for concept formation and thus the construction of cultural meaning. Instead of schematization, Hofstadter relies on the concept of "slippability," which involves subcognitive processes by which we slip out of the boundaries of one field of meaning and into another, like Alice in Wonderland or as in synesthesia. Both Shore and Hofstadter consider mimicry and memory to be key areas for investigating how analogy formation works, and both provide insightful post hoc illustrations of analogical formations, but neither can illuminate the mysterious processes by which we make analogies and, by extension, meaning. Unlike Shore, however, Hofstadter believes that we can analyze this process and eventually explain it.

To return to our initial discussion on how we recognize the squiggle as an "a," Shore would claim, I think, that we just see the "a" in the squiggle. Both Shore and Hofstadter would want to find out which cues we use to make this discrimination, but Hofstadter would want to see whether those cues can be transformed into a computational, that is, analytically explicit, algorithm, so that a computer could make the same discriminations that humans do. In this sense, Hofstadter's goal heeds Goodenough's (1956) dictum—to make explicit what we need to know in order to act appropriately in a specific situation. We still have a mighty long way to go.

Those of us who are interested in meaning are, by necessity and disposition, also interested in mystery and tolerant of ambiguity. We choose to study meaning along a "meaning continuum" anchored at one end by such questions as how humans determine that a squiggle is an "a" and at the other end by questions such as "what is the meaning of life?" We all have heard of the story of the seven blind men who touched different parts of an elephant and came up with different inferences as to what it was. The one who touched a leg called upon his image schema of a tree to infer that he was touching the massive trunk of a tree. Each part-to-whole inference was based on memory and on cultural schemas; each was reasonable given the available information; and each was wrong. Similarly, neurologists, psychologists, anthropologists, philosophers, physicists, biologists, artists, and other contemplative people look through a glass blindly to acquire partial insight into the world of meaning. No view is privileged, each is partial, and discussions need to be open and democratic. The seven blind men would have done better figuring out what was in front of their noses had they conferred with each other. The relationship between culture, self, and meaning is, in the final analysis, analogous to the golden triangle of Pythagoras: one cannot speak of one side without speaking of the other sides as well.

Notes

Chapter 2

1. Spiro (1987:6) wrote "each culture (as Ruth Benedict had argued in her seductive metaphor) has carved out a different arc from the total circle of cultural variability."

2. Similarly, Arjun Appadurai writes, "I find myself frequently troubled by the word *culture* as a noun but centrally attached to the adjectival form of the word, that is *cultural*" (1996:12).

3. The term "culture-in-general" is taken from Jonathan Spencer's discussion on Claude Lévi-Strauss (1996:141).

4. Much of this discussion was stimulated by Claudia Strauss's critique (1992a; 1997) of Geertz.

5. Cited in Strauss 1992a:10.

6. Note that my discussion here is on volitional, rather than master–slave type dyads (these are discussed in chapter 2).

7. Freeman, Roeder, and Mulholland (1980) have done a more recent version of this study.

8. I have attended two separate seminars on network analysis where this study was presented by the instructor, but I have never read the study. I also asked both instructors for citations but unfortunately they did not have them.

9. Though this statement does not, strictly speaking, encompass interpretivist approaches, all we need to do is make some minor adjustments in order for it to fit interpretivist assumptions. For example, we could define a culture as a set of scripts that are specific to the contexts that we use to write about that culture. Culture is then broken down into contexts or situations that cannot easily be combined to form a whole culture; on the other hand, each context is treated as a whole regardless of how contingent or ephemeral it may be.

Chapter 3

1. This quote and the discussion on John Locke was first found in Kurt Danzinger's excellent article "The Historical Formation of Selves" (1997).

2. The "looking-glass self" metaphor comes from Cooley (1902).

95

3. The notion of the object relation between "I" and "Me" and between "Me" and other "Mes" is crucial to the development of social, psychoanalytic and psychological theories of the self. Heinz Kohut's new school of Self psychology is based on the idea of the self being conceived of as an object by others and by the self.

4. Myers in his biography of William James wrote, "James found many things mysterious—the nature of causality, the relation between mind and body, the concepts of continuity and infinity—but he encountered nothing more resistant to conceptualization than personal identity" (cited in Modell 1993: 35–36).

5. Baldwin's concept of the relationship between self and social anticipates much of contemporary writing on the self, for example, Shweder and Bourne's view of the non-Western self as "sociocentric organic" (1984:193) and even Shore's idea of conventionalized models of culture that are "twice-born" (1996).

6. Though he does not say this, one would assume that various mood-lifting neurochemicals (e.g., phenylethylamine, an amphetamine-like compound) trigger these feelings of elation and joy (Fisher 1992).

7. I titled an article (1992) on the self "The Fallacy of the Misplaced Self" to emphasize that the self is not an entity but a discursive, and perhaps peculiarly Western, construct.

8. The choice of the term *stimulus* may be very unfortunate as it conjures up nasty behaviorist models of learning. The ideas are taken from connectionist theory, discussed in the next chapter.

9. I use the term *information gangsterism* coined, to my knowledge, by my friend Phillip Augusta.

10. The idea of language as the social system par excellence comes from de Saussure's (1959) definition of *langue*.

11. See for example Daniel (1984); Dion and Dion (1996); Gergen (1991); Kondo (1990); Markus and Kitayama (1991); Rosaldo (1980); Shweder and Bourne (1984); Shweder and Sullivan (1993); Triandis (1989).

12. Skinner, Pach and Holland (1998) formulated the "self-in-action" theory of self.

13. Erchack (1992:176) notes that Rosaldo and Lutz "devalue" Western conceptions of emotions. Bock fear(s) that Rosaldo and other social constructivists end up reinforc(ing) rather than undermining "the ethnocentric distinction between *them* (savage, primitive, emotional and oral) and *us* (civilized, individual, rational, and literate)" (1999:227).

Chapter 4

1. I first came across "slippability" in Hofstadter (1995).

2. The issue of psychological reality was critical to cognitive anthropology, particularly as the early ethnoscientists claimed that the formal methodology and analysis explicated how people actually made category discriminations. For an expanded discussion of the debate about this approach see D'Andrade 1995:48–54).

3. Most of this discussion stems from the work of my mentor, David Kronenfeld, which in turn stems from the work and ideas of his mentors, Charles Frake, Roy D'Andrade and Joseph Greenberg.

4. Kronenfeld (1996:98–100) also has a fascinating discussion on cat:cat-tomcat and dog:dog-bitch marking hierarchies.

5. See also Shore 1996 for a different but not incompatible approach to the issue of analogy formation and metaphors.

6. Six books are critical to an understanding of schema theory and cultural models in anthropology: *Scripts, Plans, Goals and Understanding,* by Roger Schank and Robert Abelson (1977); *Description and Inference,* by Ed Hutchins (1980); *Cultural Models in Language and Thought,* by Dorothy Holland and Naomi Quinn (1987); *Human Motives and Cultural Models,* by Roy D'Andrade and Claudia Strauss (1992); *A Cognitive Theory of Cultural Meaning,* by Claudia Strauss and Naomi Quinn (1997); *The Development of Cognitive Anthropology,* by Roy D'Andrade (1995).

7. This historical information and my take on Bartlett and Piaget here was derived from Linda Garro's essay "The Remembered Past in a Culturally Meaningful Life: Remembering as Cultural, Social and Cognitive Process," to appear in H. Mathews and C. Moore, eds., *The Psychology of Cultural Experience* (forthcoming).

8. See Singer and Salovey (1991) for a review of schema theory and list of definitions.

References

Abu-Lughod, L. 1986. *Veiled Sentiments*. Berkeley, CA: University of California Press.
——. 1991. Writing Against Culture. In *Recapturing Anthropology: Working in the Present*, R. D. Fox, ed. Santa Fe, NM: School of American Research Press.
Anderson, B. 1987. *Imagined Communities: Reflections on the Origins and Spread of Nationalism*. London: Verso.
Appadurai, A. 1996. *Modernity at Large: Cultural Dimensions of Globalization*. Minneapolis: University of Minnesota Press
Ashmore, R. D., and L. Jussim. 1997. *Self and Identity: Fundamental Issues*. New York: Oxford University Press.
Atran, S. 1990. *Cognitive Foundations of Natural History: Towards an Anthropology of Science*. Cambridge: Cambridge University Press.
Baars, B. J. 1997. *In the Theater of Consciousness*. New York: Oxford University Press.
Baldwin, J. M. 1968 (Orig. 1897). The Self-Conscious Person. In *The Self in Social Interaction*, C. Gordon and K. J. Gergen, eds. New York: John Wiley & Sons, Inc.
Bartlett, F. C. 1932. *Remembering: A Study in Experimental and Social Psychology*. New York: Macmillian.
Bateson, G. 1972. *Steps to an Ecology of Mind*. New York: Ballantine.
Baumeister, R. F. 1997. The Self and Society: Changes, Problems, and Opportunities. In *Self and Identity: Fundamental Issues*, R. D. Ashmore and L. Jussim, eds., pp. 191–217. New York: Oxford University Press.
Bavelas, A. 1950. Communication Patterns in Task-oriented Groups. *Journal of the Acoustical Society of America* 22:271–282.
Bechtel, W., and A. Abrahamsen. 1991. *Connectionism and the Mind: An Introduction to Parallel Processing in Networks*. Cambridge, MA.: Blackwell.
Bellah, R. N., R. Madsen, W. M. Sullivan, A. Swidler and S. M. Tipton. 1985. *Habits of the Heart*. New York: Harper and Row.
Benedict, R. 1959 (Orig. 1934). *Patterns of Culture*. Boston: Houghton Mifflin.
Berlin, B. O., and P. D. Kay. 1969. *Basic Color Terms*. Berkeley, CA: University of California Press.

Bidney, D. 1967. *Theoretical Anthropology*. New York: Columbia University Press.

Blau, P. 1977. *Inequality and Heterogeneity*. New York: Free Press.

Bock, P. K. 1999. *Rethinking Psychological Anthropology: Continuity and Change in the Study of Human Action*, 2nd ed. Prospect Heights, IL: Waveland Press.

Bohannan, P., and D. van der Elst. 1998. *Asking and Listening: Ethnography as Personal Adaptation*. Prospect Heights, IL: Waveland Press.

Bolinger, D. 1989. *Intonation and Its Uses*. Stanford, CA: Stanford University Press.

Borofsky, R. 1994. *Assessing Cultural Anthropology*. New York: McGraw-Hill.

Boster, J. 1988. Natural Sources of Internal Category Structure: Typicality, Familiarity, and Similarity of Birds. *Memory and Cognition* 16(3): 258–270.

Bourdieu, P. 1977. *Outline of A Theory of Practice*. R. Nice, trans. Cambridge: Cambridge University Press.

———. 1984. *Distinction: A Social Critique of the Judgement of Taste*. R. Nice, trans. Cambridge, MA: Harvard University Press.

———. 1991. *Language and Symbolic Power*. G. Raymond and M. Adamson, trans. Cambridge, MA: Cambridge University Press.

Brown, N. O. 1959. *Life Against Death*. New York: Vintage Books.

Brumann, C. 1999. Writing for Culture: Why a Successful Concept Should Not Be Discarded. *Current Anthropology* 40 (February): S1–S27.

Bruner, J. S. 1986. *Actual Minds, Possible Worlds*. Cambridge, MA: Harvard University Press.

Buss, D. M. 1988. Love Acts: The Evolutionary Biology of Love. In *The Psychology of Love*, R. J. Sternberg and M. L. Barnes, eds., pp. 100–118. New Haven, CT: Yale University Press.

———. 1994. *The Evolution of Desire: Strategies of Human Mating*. New York: HarperCollins.

Chomsky, N. 1986. *Knowledge of Language*. New York: Praeger.

Clifford, J. 1988. *The Predicament of Culture: Twentieth-Century Ethnography, Literature and Art*. Cambridge: Cambridge University Press.

Colby, B., and L. M. Colby. 1981. *The Daykeeper: The Life and Discourse of an Ixil Diviner*. Cambridge, MA: Harvard University Press.

Cole, M., and S. Scribner. 1974. *Culture and Thought: A Psychological Introduction*. New York: John Wiley & Sons.

Cooley, C. H. 1902. *Nature and The Social Order*. New York: Charles Scribner's Sons.

D'Andrade, R. G. 1981. A Folk Model of the Mind. In *Cultural Models in Language and Thought*, D. Holland and N. Quinn, eds., pp. 112–148. Cambridge: Cambridge University Press.

———. 1992. Schemas and Motivations. In *Human Motives and Cultural Models*, R. D'Andrade and C. Strauss, eds., pp 23–44. Cambridge: Cambridge University Press.

———. 1995. *The Development of Cognitive Anthropology*. Cambridge: Cambridge University Press.

D'Andrade, R. G., and C. Strauss, eds. 1992. *Human Motives and Cultural Models*. Cambridge: Cambridge University Press.

Daniel, V. 1984. *Fluid Signs: Being a Person the Tamil Way.* Berkeley: University of California Press.

Danzinger, K. 1997. The Historical Formation of Selves. In *Self and Identity: Fundamental Issues,* R. D. Ashmore and L. Jussim, eds., pp 137–159. New York: Oxford University Press.

de Munck, V. C. 1992. The Fallacy of the Misplaced Self: Gender Relations and the Construction of Multiple Selves Among Sri Lankan Muslims. *Ethos* 20 (1992): 167–189.

Dennett, D. 1991. *Consciousness Explained.* Boston: Little, Brown.

Dion, K. K., and K. L. Dion. 1996. Cultural Perspectives on Romantic Love. *Personal Relationships* 3(1): 5–18.

Edelman, G. 1987. *Neural Darwinism: The Theory of Neuronal Group Selection.* New York: Basic Books.

———. 1992. *Bright Air, Brilliant Fire.* New York: Basic Books.

Ekman, P. 1973. Cross-Cultural Studies of Facial Expression. In his *Darwin and Facial Expression,* pp. 169–222. New York: Academic Press.

Erchak, G. M. 1992. *The Anthropology of Self and Behavior.* New Brunswick, NJ: Rutgers University Press.

Ewing, K. P. 1990. The Illusion of Wholeness: "Culture," "Self," and the Experience of Inconsistency. *Ethos* 18:251–278.

Fehr, B., and J. A. Russell. 1991. The Concept of Love Viewed from a Prototype Perspective. *Journal of Personality and Social Psychology* 60:425–438.

Fernandez, J., and M. Herzfeld. 1998. In Search of Meaningful Methods. In *Handbook of Methods in Cultural Anthropology,* H. R. Bernard, ed., pp 89–129. Walnut Creek, CA: AltaMira Press.

Fisher, H. 1992. *The Chemistry of Love.* New York: Basic Books.

Fiske, A. 1991. *Structures of Social Life: The Four Elementary Forms of Human Relations.* New York: Free Press.

Flavell, J. 1963. *The Developmental Psychology of Jean Piaget.* New York: Van Nostrand.

Fox, R. 1999. "Culture—A Second Chance?" *Current Anthropology* 40 (February).

Frake, C. O. 1969. The Ethnographic Study of Cognitive Systems. In *Cognitive Anthropology,* S. A. Tyler, ed., pp. 28–40. New York: Holt, Rinehart and Winston.

Freeman, L. C., D. Roeder, and R. R. Mulholland. 1980. Centrality in Social Networks: II. Experimental Results. *Social Networks* 2, pp. 119–141.

Friedman, J. 1994. *Cultural Identity and Global Process.* London: Sage.

Garro, L. C. n/d. The Remembered Past in a Culturally Meaningful Life: Remembering as a Cultural, Social and Cognitive Process. In *The Psychology of Cultural Experience,* H. Mathews and C. Moore, eds. Cambridge: Cambridge University Press.

———. 1994. Narrative Representations of Chronic Illness Experience: Cultural Models of Illness, Mind, and Body in Stories Concerning the Temporomandibular Joint (TMJ). *Social Science and Medicine* 38:771–774.

Geertz, C. 1973. *The Interpretation of Cultures: Selected Essays by Clifford Geertz.* New York: Basic.

———. 1984. From the Native's Point of View. In *Cultural Theory: Essays on Mind, Self and Emotion,* R. Shweder and R. LeVine, eds., pp.123–136. Cambridge: Cambridge University Press.

Gergen, K. 1991. *The Saturated Self.* New York: Basic Books.

Goffman, E. 1959. *The Presentation of Self in Everyday Life.* New York: Doubleday.

Goodenough, W. H. 1956. Componential Analysis and the Study of Meaning. *Language* 32:195–216.

Gordon, C., and K. J. Gergen. 1968. *The Self in Social Interaction; Vol. 1, Classic and Contemporary Perspective.* New York: John Wiley & Sons.

Gramsci, A. 1971. *Selections from the Prison Notebooks of Antonio Gramsci.* Q. Hoare and G. Smith, trans. and eds. New York: International Publishers.

Granovetter, M. S. 1973. The Strength of Weak Ties. *American Journal of Sociology* 78:347–367.

Greenberg, J. 1966. *Language Universals.* The Hague: Mouton and Co.

Hallowell, A. I. 1950. Personality Structure and the Evolution of Man. *American Anthropologist* 52:159–173.

———. 1955. *Culture and Experience.* Philadelphia: University of Pennsylvania Press.

Hannerz, U. 1996. *Transnational Connections: Cultures, People, Places.* London: Routledge.

Harris, G. G. 1989. Concepts of Individual, Self, and Person in Description and Analysis. *American Anthropologist* 91:599–612.

Harter, S. 1997. The Personal Self in Social Context: Barriers to Authenticity. In *Self and Identity: Fundamental Issues,* R. D. Ashmore and L. Jussim, eds., pp. 81–105. New York: Oxford University Press.

Hegal, G. 1967 (Orig. 1807). *The Phenomenology of Mind.* J. Baillie, trans. New York: Harper Torchbooks.

Hirschfeld, L. A., and S. A. Gelman. 1994. Toward a Topography of Mind: An Introduction to Domain Specificity. In *Mapping the Mind: Domain Specificity in Cognition and Culture,* L. A. Hirschfield and S. A. Gelman, eds., pp. 3–35. Cambridge: Cambridge University Press.

Hofstadter, D. R. 1985. *Metamagical Themas: Questions for the Essence of Mind and Pattern.* New York: Bantam Books.

———. 1995. *Fluid Concepts and Creative Analogies.* New York: Basic Books.

Hofstadter, D. R., and D. C. Dennett. 1981. *The Mind's I, Fantasies and Reflections on Self and Soul.* New York: Bantam Books.

Hofstede, G. 1980. *Culture's Consequences.* Beverly Hills, CA: Sage.

Hollan, D. 1992. Cross-cultural Differences in the Self. In *Journal of Anthropological Research* 48:283–300.

Holland, D. 1982. How Cultural Systems Become Desire: A Case Study of American Romance. In *Human Motives and Desires,* R. D'Andrade and C. Strauss, eds., pp. 61–89. Cambridge: Cambridge University Press.

———. 1997. Selves as Cultured: As Told by an Anthropologist Who Lacks a Soul. In *Self and Identity: Fundamental Issues,* R. D. Ashmore and L. Jussim, eds., pp. 160–190. New York: Oxford University Press.

Holland, D., and N. Quinn. 1987. *Cultural Models in Language and Thought.* Cambridge: Cambridge University Press.

Holland, D., and D. Skinner. 1987. Prestige and Intimacy. In *Cultural Models of Language and Thought,* D. Holland and N. Quinn, eds., pp. 78–111. Cambridge: Cambridge University Press.

Howard, A. 1985. Ethnopsychology and the Prospects for a Cultural Psychology. In *Person, Self, and Experience: Exploring Pacific Ethnopsychologies*, G. M. White and J. Kirkpatrick, eds., pp. 401–420. Berkeley and Los Angeles: University of California Press.

Humprey, N., and D. C. Dennett. 1991. Speaking for Ourselves: An Assessment of Multiple Personality Disorder. In *Self and Identity*, D. Kolak and R. Martin, eds., pp. 144–161. New York: Macmillan.

Huntington, S. P. 1993. The Clash of Civilizations? *Foreign Affairs* 72(3): 22–49.

———. 1996. *The Clash of Civilizations and the Remaking of World Order*. New York: Simon and Schuster.

Hutchins, E. 1980. *Culture and Inference: A Trobriand Case Study*. Cambridge, MA: Harvard University Press.

———. 1995. *Cognition in the Wild*. Cambridge, MA: MIT Press.

Ilouz, E. 1997. *Consuming the Romantic Utopia*. Berkeley and Los Angeles: University of California Press.

Ingham, J. M. 1996. *Psychological Anthropology Reconsidered*. Cambridge: Cambridge University Press.

Jackendoff, R. S. 1992. *Languages of the Mind*. Cambridge, MA: MIT Press.

James, W. 1892. *Psychology: The Briefer Course*. Notre Dame, IN: Notre Dame University Press.

Johnson, A., and R. Sackett. 1989. Direct Systematic Observation of Behavior. In *Handbook of Methods in Cultural Anthropology*, H. R. Bernard, ed., pp. 301–331. Walnut Creek, CA: AltaMira.

Kohut, H. 1977. *The Restoration of Self*. New York: International Universities Press.

Kondo, D. 1990. *Crafting Selves: Power, Gender, and Discourses of Identity in a Japanese Workplace*. Chicago: University of Chicago Press.

Kroeber, A. L. 1909. Classificatory Systems of Relationship. *Journal of the Royal Anthropological Institute* 39:77–84.

Kronenfeld, D. 1996. *Plastic Glasses and Church Fathers*. New York: Oxford University Press.

Lasch, C. 1979. *The Culture of Narcissism*. New York: Norton.

Lee, D. 1949. Being and Value in a Primitive Culture. *Journal of Philosophy* 48:401–415.

———. 1976. *Valuing the Self*. Prospect Heights, IL.: Waveland Press.

Lewis, M. 1978. *The Culture of Inequality*. Amherst: University of Massachusetts Press.

Lifton, R. J. 1993. *The Protean Self*. New York: Basic Books.

Locke, John. 1994 (orig. 1694). *An Essay Concerning Human Understanding*. Amherst, NY: Prometheus Books

Luria, A. R. 1966. *Higher Cortical Functions in Man*. New York: Basic Books.

Lutz, C. A. 1988. *Unnatural Emotions: Everyday Sentiments on a Micronesian Atoll and Their Challenge to Western Theory*. Chicago: University of Chicago Press.

Markus, H. R., and S. Kitayama. 1991. Culture and the Self: Implications for Cognition, Emotion, and Motivation. *Psychological Review* 98:224–253.

Mathews, H. n/d. *Uncovering Models of Gender From Accounts of Folk Tales*. (Unpublished manuscript).

————. 1992. The Directive Force of Morality Tales in a Mexican Community. In *Human Motives and Cultural Models*, R. D'Andrade and C. Strauss, eds., pp.127–162. Cambridge: Cambridge University Press.

Mattingly, C., and L. C. Garro. 1994. Narrative Representations of Illness and Healing. *Social Science and Medicine* 38:771–774.

McAdams, D. P. 1997. The Case for Unity in the (Post)modern Self. In *Self and Identity: Fundamental Issues*, R. Ashmore and L. Jussim, eds. Oxford: Oxford University Press.

Mead, G. H. 1968. The Genesis of the Self. In *The Self in Social Interaction*, Pp. 51–59. New York: John Wiley & Sons.

Modell, A. H. 1993. *The Private Self*. Cambridge, MA: Harvard University Press.

Neisser, U. 1967. *Cognitive Psychology*. New York: Appleton-Century-Crofts.

————. 1976. *Cognition and Reality: Principles and Implications of Cognitive Psychology*. San Francisco, CA: Freeman.

————. 1987. Concepts and Conceptual Development: Ecological and Intellectual Factors in Categorization. *Emory Symposia in Cognition*. Cambridge: Cambridge University Press.

Obeyesekere, G. 1981. *Medusa's Hair: An Essay on Personal Symbols and Religious Experience*. Chicago: University of Chicago Press.

Ochs, E., and L. Capps. 1996. Narrating the Self. *Annual Review of Anthropology* 25:19–43.

Piaget, J. 1970. *Structuralism*. C. Maschler, trans. and ed. London: Routledge & Kegan Paul.

Plato. 1961. *Plato: The Collected Dialogues*. Princeton, NJ: Princeton University Press.

Quinn, N. 1992. The Motivational Force of Self-Understanding: Evidence of Wives' Inner Conflicts. In *Human Motives and Cultural Models*, R. D'Andrade and C. Strauss, eds. Pp. 90–126. Cambridge: Cambridge University Press.

Randall, R. 1976. How Tall is the Taxonomic Tree? Some Evidence of Dwarfism. *American Ethnologist* 3:545–546.

Rosaldo, M. Z. 1980. *Knowledge and Passion: Ilongot Notions of Self and Social Life*. Cambridge: Cambridge University Press.

Rosch, E. 1975. Universals and Cultural Specifics in Human Categorization. In *Cross-Cultural Perspectives on Learning*, R. W. Brislin, S. Bochner, and W. J. Lonner, eds. Pp. 177–206. New York: John Wiley and Sons.

————. 1978. *Principles of Categorization*, E. Rosch and B. B. Lloyd, eds. Pp. 28–48. Hillsdale, NJ: Lawrence Erlbaum Associates.

Rosch, E., and L. B. Rosch. 1978. *Cognition and Categorization*. Lawrence, NJ: Erlbaum.

Rozin, P., and A. Fallon. 1987. A Perspective on Disgust. *Psychological Review* 94:23–47.

Ryle, G. 1949. *The Concept of the Mind*. London: Hutchinson.

Sanjek, R. 1990. Fieldnotes: The Making of Anthropology. Ithaca, NY: Cornell University Press.

Saussure, F. de, 1959. *A Course in General Linguistics*. W. Baskin, trans. New York: Philosophical Library.

Schank, R., and R. Abelson. 1977. *Scripts, Plans, Goals and Understanding: An Inquiry into Human Knowledge Structures*. Hillsdale, NJ: Erlbaum.

Schwartz, T. 1978. Where Is the Culture? Personality as the Locus of Culture. In *Making of Psychological Anthropology*, G. De Vos, ed., pp. 419–441. Berkeley: University of California Press.

Shore, B. 1991. Twice Born, Once Conceived: Meaning Construction and Cultural Cognition. *American Anthropologist* 93:9–27.

———. 1996. *Culture in Mind: Meaning Construction and Cultural Cognition*. New York: Oxford University Press.

Shweder, R. A. 1991. *Thinking Through Cultures: Expeditions in Cultural Psychology*. Cambridge, MA: Harvard University Press.

———. 1993. Cultural Psychology: Who Needs It? *Annual Review of Psychology* 44:497–523.

———. 1997. The Surprise of Ethnography. *Ethos* 25(2): 152–163.

Shweder, R. A., and E. J. Bourne. 1984. Does the Concept of the Person Vary Cross-Culturally? In *Culture Theory: Essays on Mind, Self and Emotion*, R. A. Shweder and R. A. LeVine, eds., pp. 158–199. Cambridge: Cambridge University Press.

Shweder, R. A., and R. A. LeVine. 1984. Anthropology's Romantic Rebellion Against the Enlightenment, Or There's More to Thinking than Reason and Evidence, in their *Culture Theory: Essays on Mind, Self and Emotion*, pp. 27–77. Cambridge: Cambridge University Press.

Shweder, R. A., and M. A. Sullivan. 1993. Cultural Psychology: Who Needs It? *Annual Review of Psychology*, 44:497–523.

Simmel, G. 1950. *The Sociology of Georg Simmel*. K. H. Wolff, ed. and trans. New York: Free Press.

Singer, I. 1994. *Pursuit of Love*. Baltimore, MD: John Hopkins University Press.

Singer, J., and P. Salovey. 1991. Organized Knowledge Structures and Personality: Person Schemas, Self-Schemas. In *Person Schemas and Maladaptive Interpersonal Behavior Patterns*, M. Horowitz, ed., pp. 33–79. Chicago: University of Chicago Press.

Skinner, D., A. Pach, and D. Holland. 1998. *Selves in Time and Place*. Oxford: Rowman & Littlefield.

Spencer, H. 1876. *Principles of Sociology*. New York: Appleton.

Spencer, J. 1996. Claude Lévi-Strauss. In *The Encyclopedia of Social and Cultural Anthropology*, A. Barnard and J. Spencer, eds., p. 141. New York: Routledge.

Sperber, D. 1996. *Explaining Culture: A Naturalistic Approach*. Oxford: Blackwell.

Spiro, M. E. 1982. Collective Representations and Mental Representations in Religious Symbol Systems. In *On Symbols in Anthropology: Essays in Honor of Harry Hoijer*, J. Maquet, ed., pp. 45–72. Malibu, CA: Udena Publications.

———. 1987. Collective Representations and Mental Representations in Religious Symbol Systems. In *Culture and Human Nature: Theoretical Papers of Melford E. Spiro*, B. Kilborne and L. Langness, eds., pp. 161–184. Chicago: University of Chicago Press.

———. 1993. Is the Western Conception of the Self "Peculiar" Within the Context of the World Cultures? *Ethos* 21:107–153.

Strauss, C. 1992a. Models and Motives. In *Human Motives and Cultural Models*, R. D'Andrade and C. Strauss, eds., pp. 1–20. Cambridge: Cambridge University Press.

———. 1992b. What Makes Tony Run? In *Human Motives and Cultural Models*, R. D'Andrade and C. Strauss, eds. pp. 197–224. Cambridge: Cambridge University Press.

———. 1997. Partly Fragmented, Partly Integrated: An Anthropological Examination of "Postmodern Fragmented Subjects." *Cultural Anthropology* 12:362–404.

Strauss, C., and N. Quinn. 1997. *A Cognitive Theory of Cultural Meaning.* Cambridge: Cambridge University Press.

Tennov, D. 1979. Love and Limerence. New York: Stein and Day.

———. 1998. Love Madness. In *Romantic Love and Sexual Behavior*, V. C. de Munck, ed., pp. 77–88. Westport, CT: Praeger Press.

Thompson, E. P. 1994. *Making History: Writings on History and Culture.* New York: W. W. Norton.

Toren, C. 1993. "Sign into Symbol, Symbol as Sign: Cognitive Aspects of a Social Process." In *Cognitive Aspects of Religious Symbolism*, P. Boyer, ed. pp. 147–164. Cambridge: Cambridge University Press.

Triandis, H. C. 1989. The Self and Social Behavior in Differing Cultural Contexts. *Psychological Review* 96(3): 506–520.

Tyler, S. A. 1969. Introduction. In *Cognitive Anthropology*, S. A. Tyler, ed., pp. 1–23. New York: Holt, Rinehart and Winston.

Tylor, E. B. 1958. *Primitive Culture: Researches Into the Development of Mythology, Philosophy, Religion, Language, Art and Custom.* London: J. Murray.

Wallace, A. F. C. 1969. The Problem of the Psychological Validity of Componenial Analyses. In *Cognitive Anthropology*, S. A. Tyler, ed., pp. 396–418. New York: Holt, Rinehart and Winston.

Wallace, A. F. C., and J. Atkins. 1969. The Meaning of Kinship Terms. In *Cognitive Anthropology*, S. A. Tyler, ed., pp. 345–369. New York: Holt, Rinehart and Winston.

Wason, P. 1968. Reasoning About a Rule. *Journal of Experimental Psychology* 20:273–281.

Whitaker, M. 1996a. Reflexivity. In *The Encyclopedia of Social and Cultural Anthropology*, A. Barnard and J. Spencer, eds., pp. 470–473. New York: Routledge.

———. 1996b. Relativism. In *The Encyclopedia of Social and Cultural Anthropology*, A. Barnard and J. Spencer, eds. pp. 478–481. New York: Routledge.

Whitehead, A. 1927. *Science in the Modern World.* Cambridge: Cambridge University Press.

Winnicott, D. W. 1958. Hate in the Countertransference. In *Collected Papers.* New York: Basic Books.

Wittgenstein, L. 1953. *Philosophical Investigations.* New York: Macmillian.

Index

107